DAVID BUTLER

BUSINESS STUDIES

D1579251

OXFORD UNIVERSITY PRESS 1989

Contents

Acknowledgements

I wish to personally acknowledge the help and assistance received in the preparation of this text from the following: *i* Peter Crane (North Tyneside College of Further Education), Colin Swansborough Accountants, Hilary Thomson (Compass Creative Consultants) and Kay Hart (National Association of Citizen Advice Bureaux). I would also like to thank my wife and family for their support during the period of writing the text.

David R. Butler

The publishers would like to thank the following for permission to reproduce photographs:

Amstrad/Michael Joyce Consultants 85 (centre right);
Baker-Britt 200 (top), 201 (top left and right);
Baltic Exchange 200 (bottom);
Bank of England 137 (top);
Bolton Business Ventures 33, 47, 108, 109 (top), 110, 144 (top);
Bolton Metropolitan Borough Planning Dept. 136 (bottom left);
Boots 85 (bottom left);
Bradford Economic Development Unit 136 (top left and bottom right);
Brighton Borough Council Technical Services 205 (centre right), 213;
Brighton Resort Services 207 (top right);
British Airways 197 (centre left);
British Coal 205 (bottom right);
British Rail 199*, 207 (bottom right);
British Telecom 125 (bottom), 126;
British Waterways Board 197 (bottom right);
Brooke Bond Oxo 188 (bottom right);
Cambridgeshire Corporate Policy and Planning 136 (top right);
CEGB 205 (lower centre right);
Consumers' Association 196;
Fiona Corbridge 169, 205 (top);
Debenhams 81;
Mary Evans Picture Library 189 (top);
Financial Times 139 (left and right), 140 (bottom), 179;
Freightliners 197 (top right), 201 (centre);
ICI 85 (centre left);
International Stock Exchange Photo Library 137 (bottom);
Lever Bros/Cull Photographic 86 (left and centre left);
National Exhibition Centre 224 (bottom);
Network/John Sturrock 168 (centre and bottom right), 205 (centre left);
Northshore Yacht Yards 140 (top);
Nuclear Electricity Information Group 188 (top left);
Alan Owens 22, 104, 109 (bottom), 142, 144 (top), 145, 148, 156, 173, 174, 175 (bottom);
P & O 201 (bottom left);
Panasonic Industrial UK 125 (top);
Simon Platt 44;
The Post Office 165, 207 (bottom left);
Procter & Gamble 86 (right and centre right);
Report/Stefano Cagnoni 168 (bottom left), 205 (bottom left), 207 (top left),/John Harris 168 (top right), 175 (top), 224 (lower centre),/John Smith 168 (top left);
Rowntree 99, 186;
Shell 85 (bottom right), 139 (centre);
Small Firms Centre, HMSO Crown Copyright 224 (top);
Stagetruck 197 (top left);
Swish 188 (bottom left);
TDK UK Ltd 188 (top right);
Training Commission, Crown Copyright 159, 224 (upper centre);
Trusthouse Forte 228;
Virgin/Laister Dickson 85 (top), 87;
World Ship Society 197 (centre right);

The 'portrait' photos have been posed by models.

The illustrations are by Peter Ahern, Nancy Anderson, Carr Associates, Caroline della Porta, Clive Goodyer, Mark Hackett, Sue Heap, Beverly Levy, Ch'en Ling, Mark Rogerson, Cheryl Tarbuck, Borin Van Loon and Gary Wing.

Preface

This book is for students preparing for the GCSE examination in Business Studies and will also be useful for related courses. The text has taken account of both the National Criteria for Business Studies and all SEAC approved business studies syllabuses. The text and exercises have been trialled with a mixed ability group of GCSE business studies students in a comprehensive school.

The approach wherever possible is student centred and places emphasis on the development of key concepts through case studies and exercises. After a brief introductory section, the student is first introduced to basic business ideas through the small firm. This approach has proved to be successful as the student can more easily identify with the small business unit in the early stages of the course. Many of these ideas are then developed in relation to the large firm in Section III, while new concepts are also introduced. The final section of the book deals with wider issues and looks at the relationship between the state and business activity.

The teaching aims are clearly identified at the start of each unit and there is a summary of key words and ideas at the end of each unit. Apart from the activities, questions and exercises within the body of the text, there are test questions at the end of each unit as well as suggestions for coursework assignments. The questions are designed to test understanding of ideas rather than factual recall and are structured for the full ability range.

The main body of the text is targeted at average-ability students and there has been a deliberate effort to avoid the use of too much unnecessary jargon. The book does also contain all that is required by the most able students in order to obtain the highest possible grades. Some sections of the book are marked as 'extension' sections where the ideas are regarded as more difficult or not essential to the 'core' needs of most syllabuses. Extension questions have been included at the end of each unit in order to test the more able student.

Section I

An introduction to business

Unit 1   The nature and purpose of business activity

aims   At the end of this unit you should understand:

▶   The terms *consumer* and *producer*.
▶   How businesses try to supply the needs and wants of consumers.
▶   The idea of opportunity cost.
▶   The chain of production and the need for the *primary*, *secondary* and *tertiary* sectors in the economy.
▶   The factors of production.
▶   The nature of the working population and how it has changed.
▶   The different types of economies: *planned*, *market*, *mixed*.

Consumer needs and wants

exercise

A *consumer* is anyone who buys *goods* and *services*. A good is any item produced for sale, such as a bar of chocolate, a car, or a washing machine. A service is where a business performs work for customers, such as hairdressing, window cleaning and dry cleaning.

1 List the pictures shown on page 2 under the heading of either Goods or Services.

2 Different consumers have different wants. For each picture, say what type of person is most likely to want the good or service. (Male? Female? Child? Teenager? Adult? Senior Citizen? Everyone?)

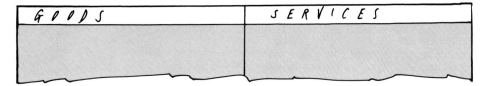

GOODS	SERVICES

Scarcity and choice

exercise

A rich uncle has just died and has left you £1000 in his will.

1 Name four goods or services you would spend the money on.

2 If you inherited a further £1000 would you
   a buy more of the same goods or services as before or,
   b buy different goods and services?

Because resources (in this case the £2000) are scarce, we have to make choices between wants. In choosing four goods or services you automatically gave up other possibilities.

The opportunity cost of a good or service is what you have to give up to obtain it in terms of the next best alternative. The opportunity cost of a hamburger may be two portions of chips. The opportunity cost of watching television may be not reading a book.

The basic economic problem of making choices between different needs and wants faces consumers, firms and countries.

● A consumer needs to make choices about what goods and services to buy on a given income.

● Firms need to make choices about what to produce and how to produce it with a given set of resources. They may need to make a choice, for example, between employing more workers or buying a new machine. A farmer may need to choose between growing wheat or barley in a particular field.

● Countries need to decide what to produce with the labour supply and resources available to them. They also need to make decisions about who gets what — should the production of goods and services be shared equally or unequally?

The chain of production

The chain of production for a bar of chocolate

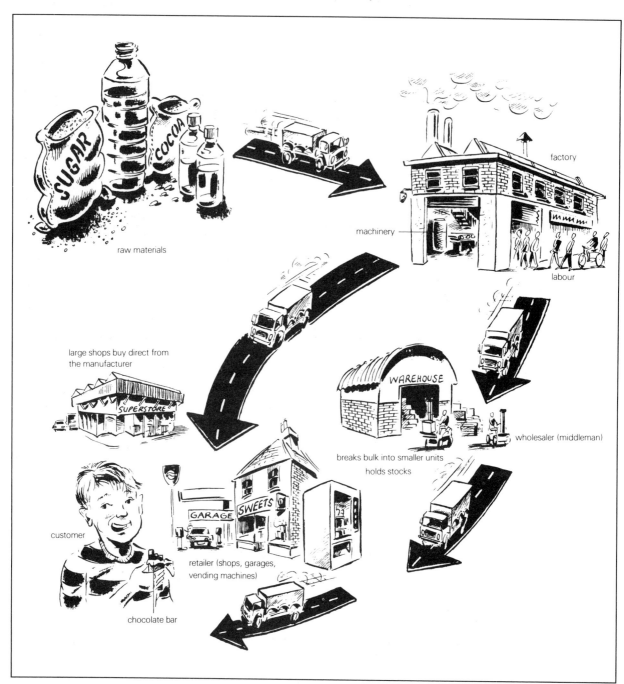

exercise Draw *chain of production* diagrams for

a a bottle of milk,

b a pair of jeans.

Types of economic activity

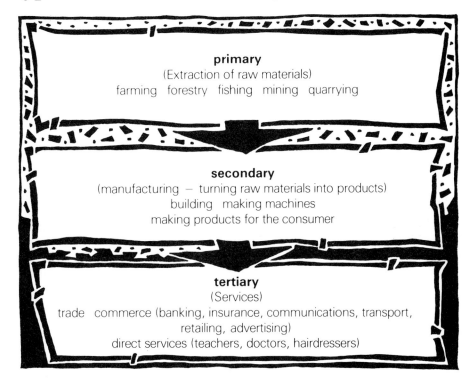

primary
(Extraction of raw materials)
farming forestry fishing mining quarrying

secondary
(manufacturing — turning raw materials into products)
building   making machines
making products for the consumer

tertiary
(Services)
trade   commerce (banking, insurance, communications, transport,
retailing, advertising)
direct services (teachers, doctors, hairdressers)

exercise

1 Write down the three types of economic activity: Primary, Secondary and Tertiary. List each of the following activities under the correct heading: Lloyds Bank, dentist, British Coal, Ford Motor Company, British Steel Corporation, Marks and Spencer, London Brick Company, British Gas, British Telecom, Shell Oil, Hilton Hotels, Heinz.

2 Explain why some of the activities listed above could be considered under more than one heading.

The factors of production

The scarce resources required to produce goods and services can be divided into three groups:

- *Land* this includes not only areas of land but also raw materials, such as minerals and chemicals.

- *Labour* the workforce, including manual labour (people working with their hands), office workers and managers.

- *Capital* the buildings, machinery and equipment used to produce goods. The word *capital* is also used to describe finance, such as loans and shares — these are examined in Unit 8).

How the factors of production are employed to produce a pair of jeans

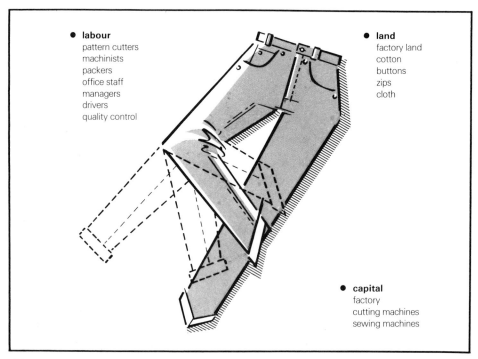

- **labour**
  pattern cutters
  machinists
  packers
  office staff
  managers
  drivers
  quality control

- **land**
  factory land
  cotton
  buttons
  zips
  cloth

- **capital**
  factory
  cutting machines
  sewing machines

exercise   Choose any simple product and construct a diagram similar to the one above to show how the factors of production are used to produce it.

The working population

The working population is all those people who are in work or who offer themselves for work (it therefore includes the unemployed). The total population of the UK is 56·5 million (1987) and the working population is approximately 26 million. An important trend in the last 20 years has been the growing number of women in the working population — they now account for 40% of the total.

The size of the working population depends upon:

- The total size of the population.

- The age of retirement.

- The school leaving age.

- The number of people in education beyond the age of 16.

- The age distribution of population (the number of people in each age group).

- The sex distribution of population (the ratio of males to females).

Changes in the working population			
	1966 %	1976 %	1986 %
Primary	6	3	3
Secondary	46	39	33
Tertiary	48	58	64

exercise

1 Represent the above figures by bar charts.

2 Describe how the working population has changed in the last 20 years.

3 Why do you think these changes have occurred?

extension section

De-industrialisation

In the last 20 years there has been a decline in the number of jobs in manufacturing in the UK both in actual numbers and in the percentage of the total workforce. Between 1979 and 1986 there was a loss of two million jobs in manufacturing. This has been called *de-industrialisation*. Why has this occurred? Economists disagree as to the exact cause. Suggested reasons include:

- New technology has meant less need for workers in manufacturing, machines have been taking over more and more jobs.

- A modern economy requires more services, such as banking, insurance and leisure industries.

- Foreign competition has made it more difficult to sell UK manufactured goods abroad. At the same time, the UK is buying more manufactured goods from other countries.

- There has been a growth in services provided by the government and local government in the last 20 years, including health, social services and education.

Although there has been a decline in the total number of jobs in manufacturing, some manufacturing industries have been expanding and employing more people. These *growth industries* include the making of electronic components and computers, as well as food processing.

There have also been changes within the service industries, with some types of employment expanding and others declining. There has been a growth of employment in such industries as information technology, finance and leisure pursuits, and a decline in employment in transport and domestic service.

Describe how technical changes have affected shops and offices in the last 20 years. Explain how these changes might affect the nature of employment in these two areas. Have they helped to increase or decrease jobs? How will the type of work being done change?

Types of economy

All countries throughout the world are faced with the same basic economic problem — how to use their scarce resources and how to share out the goods and services produced by these resources.

case study

You and a group of friends are shipwrecked on a desert island. Because of your charm, high intelligence and leadership qualities, you are elected as the supreme ruler of the island.

a What basic needs would you try to meet first in order to survive the first week?

A month has gone by and you have all survived — well done!

b What 'luxury' goods or services would you now try to produce?

After 6 months on the island only one person has died (as a result of a falling coconut) but you and your friends are getting bored with a diet of fish and coconuts. One day there is great excitement: a case of tins of baked beans is washed ashore. You immediately order them to be put in your hut until you are able to decide how to share them out.

You are now faced with the basic economic problem. You have scarce resources (the tins of baked beans) and you need to decide how to share them out amongst competing wants (your friends). You jot down the following ideas in the sand:

● Share them out equally.

● Share them out according to each person's needs, eg big people get more than small people.

● Put a price on each tin in terms of so many hours work to be done.

● Keep most of them yourself and give the rest to the strongest people to protect you from the likely uprising.

What are the advantages and disadvantages of each method of sharing out the tins?

Planned economies

mixed economies
eg UK, France

free-market economies
eg USA, Japan

planned economies
eg USSR, China

The desert island case study on the previous page is an example of a planned, or centrally controlled, economy. The central authority (you in this case) controlled the sharing out of resources and decided what goods and services would be produced. In the USSR the state controls the factors of production and decides what goods and services will be produced and how they will be allocated amongst consumers.

- The state can decide upon an order of priorities for the whole community and try to provide benefit for all the population. It may, for example, decide that resources are better used to provide health care and education than luxury consumer items.

- Wasteful competition may be avoided and factors of production can be fully used. Unemployment, for example, can be avoided because the state owns and controls all the means of production.

- There are no private monopolies which might use their power to exploit the consumer. (A monopoly is where one firm controls most of the output.)

- Firms are not producing for profit and may therefore be able to take account of such problems as pollution and the effects on the local community.

- The lack of competition caused by the state owning all means of production may lead to a lack of efficiency and inventiveness.

- Because the main aim is not profit, there may be a lack of incentive to improve both as an individual and as a firm.

- It is very difficult to calculate the needs of the population and this may result in either under- or over-production.

- Central planning may restrict the economic freedom of the individual.

Free-market economies

free-market
economies
and mixed
economies

A pure free market economy is one where there is no state ownership of the means of production. The state does not determine what is produced and how resources are allocated. This is done through the price system. Prices reflect the demand for a good or service in relation to its supply. Increased demand for a product will result in its price rising. The higher price will encourage more firms to produce the good because they can make more profit. If there is a surplus of a product the price will have to fall in order to sell the good.

**advantages of
free-market
economies**

- Competition and the opportunity to make large profits may result in greater efficiency and more innovations.
- The price system helps to match demand and supply so that shortages and surpluses may be avoided.
- People are free to take part in business activities for the purpose of profit.

**disadvantages
of free-market
economies**

- Competition may be wasteful.
- The market may not produce essential services if they do not make a profit.
- Private monopolies may exploit the consumer by controlling output and sales.

Mixed economies

- In reality few economies are either purely free market or totally centrally controlled. In the USSR there is a considerable amount of free enterprise. In the USA there is some state involvement in business. When we refer to free market or planned economies we usually mean that the way in which resources are allocated comes very close to being one of the two types.
- Mixed economies involve aspects of both free market and centrally planned economies. In the UK, for example, the state owns a considerable share of enterprise, but most of it is in the hands of the private sector. Prices largely control the allocation of resources in the private sector.
- The balance between the public and private sectors depends upon government policy. The current Conservative government has reduced

the size of the public sector by 'privatising' industries such as British Telecom and British Gas.

- The remainder of this book is concerned mainly with the UK and is set in the context of the mixed economy.

Summary of key words and ideas

- A *consumer* is a buyer of goods and services.
- A *producer* is a firm making goods or supplying services.
- Consumers, firms and nations are all concerned with the basic economic problem of how to allocate scarce resources.
- *Opportunity cost* is what needs to be given up in order to obtain a particular good or service.
- The *chain of production* is the various stages involved in producing a good.
- The *wholesaler* is the middleman between the manufacturer and the retailer. (shop).
- *Primary activity* is concerned with the extraction of raw materials.
- *Secondary activity* is manufacturing — turning the raw materials into finished goods.
- *Tertiary activity* is concerned with providing services.
- The *factors of production* are the 'ingredients' needed to make a particular good. They include *Land* (land itself and raw materials), and *Labour and Capital* (machinery, tools, buildings and equipment)
- The *working population* is all those people who are at work or who offer themselves for employment.
- The last 20 years have seen a decline in the numbers employed in the secondary sector and a growth in the numbers employed in services.
- *Deindustrialisation* is the decline in the number of workers employed in manufacturing industry.
- A *planned* or *centrally controlled* economy is one where the state owns and controls the means of production.
- A *free-market economy* is one where the means of production are owned privately and resources are allocated through the price system.
- A *mixed economy* contains elements of both the free market and planned economies.

Test questions

1 'All countries are faced with the basic economic problem of how to share out scarce resources between competing needs.'
   a What is meant by 'scarce resources'?
   b What is meant by 'competing needs?'
   c Describe two different ways a country might try to share out its resources and state one advantage and one disadvantage of each method.

2 a Complete the following chain of production diagram for a tin of tomatoes:

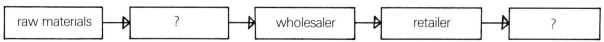

| raw materials | → | ? | → | wholesaler | → | retailer | → | ? |

b What is a wholesaler?
c What is a retailer?

Employment in Radshire 1967–1987			
% of Employment in:	1967	1977	1987
Primary sector	5	3	3
Secondary sector	60	50	40
Tertiary sector	30	40	50
Unemployment	5	7	7
Working population (000's)	400	410	420

a Give two examples of jobs in each of the primary, secondary and tertiary sectors.
b Describe the main changes shown in the table.
c To what extent are the changes shown in the table similar or different to the changes in the UK's working population in the last 20 years?
d Calculate the number of people in each sector in 1987 (show your working).
e Give two possible reasons why the working population has increased in size.
4 List the following resources under the correct factor of production (Land, Labour and Capital):
cement mixer, secretary, sugar, coal, building land, factory, driver, manager, screwdriver, scissors.

Extension questions

1 There has been a considerable decline in the number of manufacturing jobs in the UK during the last 20 years.
   a Suggest three reasons why this has occurred.
   b Name one manufacturing industry that has not declined and suggest why this is the case.
   c Which sector of the economy has seen an increase in jobs? Give two possible reasons why this has happened.
2 Describe two differences between a centrally planned economy such as the USSR and a free market economy such as the U.S.A.
3 The UK is described as a 'mixed economy'. Explain what is meant by this term.
4 Both free market and centrally planned economies are faced with the problem of how to allocate scarce resources between competing needs. Explain how each type of economy attempts to deal with this problem.

Section II

The small business

Unit 2   Setting up

aims   At the end of this unit you should understand:

- ▶ Why small businesses are set up.
- ▶ Why some small businesses are a success and others are a failure.
- ▶ What we mean by a *market*.
- ▶ The purpose and meaning of *market research*.
- ▶ The advantages and disadvantages of small businesses.

Starting a small business

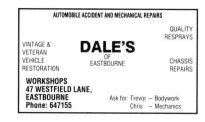

French Polishing
Furniture Repaired and
Re-polished.
Antique or modern.
Free estimates.
Polegate 5222

BABY SITTING SERVICE
Sitters for most areas.
Excellent references. Responsible adults
Call office hours for details 646994

PROFESSIONAL PHOTOGRA-
PHY for Weddings, portraits and
special occasions. Wendy Hooper,
844894.

F.C. LLOYD
GENERAL HOUSE AND GARDEN WORK
PATIOS, PATHS, CANOPIES, FENCING,
CONCRETE BASES, PERGOLAS ETC.
Other Enquiries Welcome
EVENINGS TELEPHONE 607744

These are just a few examples of the estimated one and a quarter million small businesses in the UK. Firms with less than 200 employees account for about 25% of the total work force — although they only produce about 15% of total output in the UK.

A great number of these firms, like the ones in the examples, employ less than 20 people and many of them are 'one-man' businesses.

Each year a large number of new businesses are started. Some of these are successful and a few go on to become much larger organisations. Many new businesses, however, fail to survive and disappear after a few months.

Businesses are often started by people who have worked for others and now want the opportunity to 'go it alone'. They feel that they will gain more satisfaction from being their own boss and controlling their own affairs. There is always the chance too of making more money in the future than they might get from working for someone else. In the last few years many businesses have been started by people out of work using redundancy money and help from the government to set up. Some businesses have also been started by school and college leavers who have found difficulty in getting the types of jobs they want at the end of their education.

Be your own boss

Have you got what it takes to set up your own business?

The first thing is to start with a really good idea. You must think of a product or service that you can sell to other people. There must be consumers willing to buy whatever it is you are providing. We call this finding a *market* for the product or service. You might think of something completely new — such as a new board game or toy. In this case you will need to create your own market for your invention. More probably you will choose something which is being done already. Here there will be an existing market and you will need to compete with firms doing the same basic idea.

Have another look at the advertisements on the previous page and ask yourself what the market is for each good or service being provided. You will get some more ideas by looking through your own local newspapers. Whatever you choose, it must not involve expensive equipment or premises. In this assignment you are limited to £500 to start up with and the use of the garden shed if you need it.

tasks

1 Invent a name for your business.
2 Briefly describe your idea.
3 Describe the market for your product or service. (Say who you think will be your customers.)
4 Why do you think your business will be a success? What competition will you face?

---

case study

Klippers

Karen left school at sixteen and went to the local College of Further Education where she took a course in hairdressing. At the end of the course she was taken on part-time at a large hairdressers in the town. She gained some useful experience and eventually got a full-time job at a small shop near where she lived. After two years of working she was becoming bored and felt that there were few promotion prospects. She wanted to set up on her own but was unable to raise enough finance to buy or rent a shop. She then had the idea of cutting people's hair in their own house. Many old people in the area found it difficult getting to the hairdressers and other people, such as mothers with young children, found it hard to get out of the house during the day.

Karen had managed to save enough out of her wages to buy the basic equipment, such as razors and driers, as well as a small stock of shampoos, conditioners, colourants and other materials. She was also the proud owner of a small car which she had bought after passing her test.

She started off by working in the evenings cutting the hair of friends and relatives and worked full time at the shop during the day. After six months she had managed to build up enough business to give up her job at the shop and to work just for herself.

After a year Karen is still in business. She finds it very hard work because she needs to work the hours that suit her customers. Business also varies and some weeks she is left with less money than her earnings at the shop. Despite this, Karen likes working for herself and hopes that she can eventually make enough money to get her own shop.

questions

1 Is Karen's business a service or a manufacturing business?
2 How did Karen raise enough money to start her business?
3 What was the market for Karen's business? (Who were her customers?)
4 Why do you think Karen has been successful in staying in business so far?
5 Karen often works longer hours and takes home less pay than she did working at the shop. Why do you think she wants to work for herself?
6 Suggest three ways in which Karen could possibly improve her business in the future.

extension exercise

We saw in Unit I (page 5) that businesses need to use combinations of the factors of production: land (materials), labour and capital. Klippers is no exception. Think of all the items Karen would need in her business and then divide them into Land and Capital.

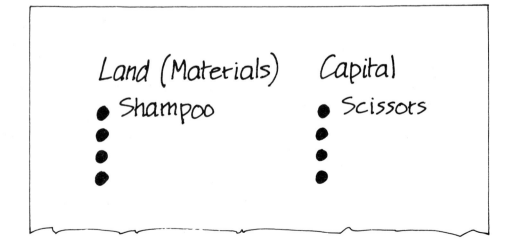

Land (Materials)
● Shampoo
●
●
●

Capital
● Scissors
●
●
●

Why do businesses fail?

Karen has already done better than many new businesses which fail in less than a year. Why do so many businesses fail?

- The idea is not good enough
- There is not a large enough market for the product or service.
- The firm runs short of finance even though it has orders. (This might be a 'cash flow problem' — see Unit 5, page 48–49)
- The owner of the firm might lack the correct business skills — they might not keep the accounts correctly for example.
- The firm might lose its market because of competition from other firms.

You might be able to add to this list by thinking of businesses that have failed in your area. In later units we will be looking in more detail at some of the problems that businesses face. The following case study shows several of the reasons for businesses failing.

---

case study **Pips**

Simon and John left school at sixteen without jobs. After six months of being unemployed and with little chance of finding suitable employment, they decided to have a go at setting up their own business. They had learnt a bit about printing at school and with the help of an interest-free loan from Simon's dad, they managed to buy a second-hand printing press together with letters and plates. They called their business 'Personalised Ink Printing Services', or PIPS for short.

At first they did quite well with orders from friends and relatives for headed note paper, invitations and business cards. Before Christmas they had great difficulty keeping up with all the orders — they even had to turn some customers away because they knew they would be unable to complete orders intended as Christmas presents.

Despite being very busy, Simon and John dicovered that they had made very little money from their work before Christmas. Simon's dad suggested that they had not charged enough for their work and that they needed a bigger 'mark up' in order to increase their profits. So Simon and John increased their prices. Things went from bad to worse though. Now they had trouble getting orders. They were told that it was cheaper to get work done by Express Printers, a large organisation in the city. Simon and John knew that Express Printers handled a huge number of orders and had the most up-to-date printing equipment, but they were still puzzled by their low prices. Express Printers needed to rent a large building for their work and to pay a large number of workers. Then a friend of John's dad, who worked at Express Printers, told them that Express printers managed to get their paper at almost half the price that John and Simon needed to pay.

1 List all the problems faced by Simon and John's business.
2 How were Simon and John caught in a trap over what prices to charge?
3 How was Express Printers able to 'undercut' PIPS?
4 Why do you think Express Printers were able to obtain their paper at almost half the price paid by Simon and John?
5 What advice could you offer to Simon and John to help their business survive?

	PIPS	Express Printers
Cost of paper per 100 sheets	£3	£1.60
Other costs per 100 sheets (not including wages)	£2	£2.40
Selling price per 100 sheets	£7	£6
Mark up (selling price *less* costs) per 100 sheets	—	—
% Mark up $\left(\dfrac{\text{Mark up}}{\text{Costs}} \times \dfrac{100}{1} \right)$	—	—

a Complete the table
b What conclusions can you draw from the table?

Market research

- How do you know your product will sell?
- Who will buy your product?
- Have you got the right design?
- Is the price right?
- Why are you losing sales to your competitors?

A firm can find some of the answers to these questions through *market research*. Market research means finding out what people want in a product or service. Large firms will often spend very large sums of money on market research, but small firms may also find it useful. Some small firms fail because they have not carried out at least some basic market research.

Market research is normally carried out through using a questionnaire. Because it is difficult and expensive to ask all your possible customers, the survey is usually carried out on a sample of people. This might be a *random sample* where, for example, you ask every tenth person regardless of whether they are male or female, young or old. On the other hand, you might select your sample so that you deliberately ask particular groups of people, males age 18–25 or females over the age of 30, for example.

**market
research
exercise**

Sax Ltd

〜〜〜 SAX LTD. 〜〜〜

Clarke House, Dreyfuss Street, Crimpton, Bucks CN3 1QT
Telephone: Crimpton 7432/3/4

Sax Ltd are a small firm making different types of nylon bags.
They want to launch a new bag which they hope will be used
by school and college students. They have come up with four
possible designs each of which could be produced in four
different colours. Firms find it very expensive to produce a large
range, particularly if one particular design or colour does not
sell well. Sax want to find out which two designs would be most
popular and which two colours students would most want to see
available. There are also a number of special features, such as
zip pockets, separate compartments, name tags, etc, which can
be added at extra cost.

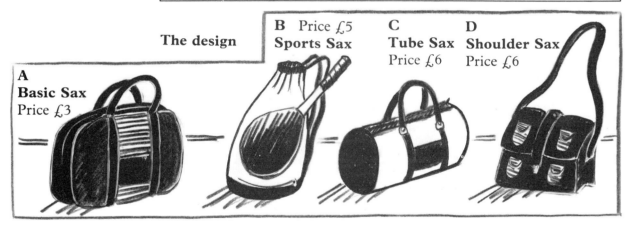

The design

B Price £5
Sports Sax

C
Tube Sax
Price £6

D
Shoulder Sax
Price £6

A
Basic Sax
Price £3

Colours   Each design available in *red, blue, green, pink*

method

This exercise is best done working in a group of about four or five
students. Each member of the group asks at least five students to
complete the questionnaire. It is best if you are able to ask a range of
students: males/females, and different ages.
When you have each collected the information, put it all together to
find out:

1 The top two designs.
2 The two colours these designs are most required in.
3 Which additional features are required (if any).
4 A customer 'profile' for each of the two designs picked. Who will be
   the most likely buyer? Male/female? Age range?

Market research sheet

MARKET RESEARCH SHEET		1	2	3	4	5	6	7	8
AGE(YEARS)	11–13								
	14–16								
	17–18								
MALE(M)FEMALE(F)	M								
	F								
DESIGN(A,B,C,or D)									
COLOUR(R,B,G,or P)									
ADDITIONAL FEATURES; (MORE THAN 1 POSSIBLE)									
(tick)Zip Pocket(+£1)									
Compartment(+£1)									
Name Tag(+50p)									

extension exercise

1 Compare the group results with the rest of the class. Have other groups come up with the same two designs? If their results are different, can you discover why?

2 Carry out your own market research in the same way. It could be to decide on which flavour packets of crisps or chocolate bars to stock in a school or college shop, for example.

3 How would the type of market research vary according to the product or service in question? For example, how would market research for an industrial vacuum cleaner be different from a soap powder?

Summary of key words and ideas

- Small businesses are those employing less than 200 people. Many of these employ less than 20 people.
- One out of every four workers is employed in a small firm.
- Small firms account for about 15% of all output in the UK.
- *The market* is the number of people willing to buy a particular product or service.
- In order to survive, firms must have a big enough market for their product or service.
- People who own their businesses and work for themselves get satisfactions from this apart from money.
- *Mark up* is the amount a firm adds on to its costs in order to fix its price.
- *Market research* is finding out what people want in the way of new or existing products and services.
- *A random sample* is when a certain number of people are asked about their wants regardless of their age, sex, income, etc.
- Different people have differing wants and requirements from goods and services.

Suggestions for coursework

a Using local newspapers, pick out twenty small businesses.

- Group them into services or manufacturers.
- Say what market each one is trying to supply.
- For any four of them say whether or not you think they will be successful in the future, giving your reasons.

b Interview the owners of at least two small businesses to try to find out:

- Why they set up their own businesses.
- What they did before they set up on their own.
- What satisfactions they get from running their own businesses.
- What problems they faced when they first started in business and what they consider to be their main problems now.

c Imagine that you are going to set up a small business in your local area. Design a questionnaire and carry out market research to establish whether your business is likely to be a success. Include a description of the type of sample you used and the results of your research.

d For the business identified in c above, draw up a basic business plan, including what the business will be doing, how you are going to organise it, who you will be selling to and any problems you are likely to face.

Test questions

1 Name any two small businesses in your area. Describe what each business does. State whether each business is a service or manufacturing business.
2 What is meant by the *market* for a good or service? What is the market for a corner shop?
3 Tracey and Jon intend to set up a clothes shop in the town of Norton. They are advised by a friend to carry out some *market research* before starting the business.
   a What is meant by market research?
   b Describe four things they might hope to discover from their market research.
   c Give two reasons why they might want to set up their own business.
4 Many small businesses fail in their first two years. Give four reasons why so many small businesses fail to survive.

Focus on Business

Success story for Joiner Jim

Joiner Jim Smith from Huddersfield left working for a local firm of builders over a year ago and is now making a success of it on his own. Jim is making high quality, custom-built tables, chairs and cabinets. 'Many people are moving away from cheap stuff and back to really well built, solid wood – and they are prepared to pay for it.' Jim is not trying to compete with the large manufacturers – they are cheaper and better at producing standardised furniture.

Jim has a full order book for the next six months and has taken on extra help. But it wasn't always like that. Jim is the first to tell you that there were plenty of problems in the first few months and that he often works harder and takes home less pay than in his old job . . .

5 a What is the market for Jim's firm?
   b Why do you think that the large manufacturers are cheaper at producing standardised furniture?
   c Give two reasons why Jim might gain satisfaction from being his own boss.
   d Describe *three* problems that Jim might have faced in the first few months of his new business.

Extension questions

1 'Small businesses can sometimes find *a gap in the market* left by large firms'. Explain what this means and give an example of it.
2 A local bus company wishes to find out whether it would be profitable to set up a new route between a housing estate and a shopping centre. Explain in detail how the bus company could attempt to find out this information.

3

Comparison of prices between a 'corner shop' and large supermarket February 1988

	Corner shop (pence)	Supermarket (pence)
Tin of baked beans (447 grams)	29	27 (own brand)
Sugar (kilo)	58	54
Milk (pint)	27	27
Potatoes (lb)	9	10

  a What do the above figures show?
  b Explain the above figures.
  c Give *two* possible reasons why people still use the 'corner shop' even though the supermarket is cheaper for most goods.
4 'The motor car industry is dominated by a few very large firms such as Ford or General Motors, yet small firms such as Jaguar still manage to survive'
  a Why do you think the car industry is 'dominated by a few very large firms?'
  b How do small firms in the car industry manage to survive?
  c Name another industry with a large number of small firms and explain why you think they have survived.

Unit 3   What type of business organisation?

aims   At the end of this unit you should understand:

▶   What is meant by *limited* and *unlimited liability*.
▶   The need for different types of business organisations.
▶   How small businesses can be set up as sole owners, partnerships, private limited companies and cooperatives.
▶   The advantages and disadvantages of each type of business organisation.

Limited or unlimited?

Some businesses have the letters *Ltd* after their name. This stands for *limited liability*. (In Unit 8 we consider the PLC — public limited company, a form of business organisation used by large firms which also gives limited liability). Owners of firms having limited liability are only responsible for debts up to the value of the business. If a firm does not have limited liability, we say that it has *unlimited liability*. This means that the owner is personally responsible for all the debts of the firm. All sole owners and most partnerships have unlimited liability.

1 The sad story of builder Fred Jones

Fred Jones set up as a self-employed builder and decorator three years ago. Things went well for Fred at first and he started taking on other workers to help him. Unfortunately, whilst working on a property, one of Fred's workers punctured a water main and caused several thousand pounds damage. Fred hired most of his equipment and he did not have the necessary cash in the business to pay for the damage. The result was that Fred had to sell his most prized possession, his vintage sports car, in order to raise the cash.

Fred had unlimited liability so his personal property was at risk: in this case it was his car, but it could have included his house and savings.

2 The collapse of Jo Jeans Ltd

In July 1986 Jo Jeans Ltd, a small firm making high-fashion jeans, went bankrupt. At the time of going bankrupt Jo Jeans Ltd owed £2000 to their suppliers and had a loan from the bank of £5000.

A 'receiver' was called in to arrange for the debts to be settled by selling off all of the property belonging to Jo Jeans (known as the assets of the business). This included their stock, machinery, van, etc. All this amounted to only £6000. The bank had first claim on this money and the suppliers were left being owed £1000. Jo Jeans had limited liability, so only the value of the business was at risk.

questions

1 Which business had limited liability and which was unlimited?
2 Name four local businesses which have *Ltd* after their name.
3 What problems did unlimited liability create?
4 Who lost out through limited liability?

extension exercise

You will see later that getting limited liability costs money and involves the firm in keeping accurate records and accounts. For which types of businesses do you think it is desirable to have limited liability and for which types do you think it is not worth bothering with? Explain your answer.

Types of business organisation

There are a number of different types of business organisations depending on how the firm is owned. In this unit we are going to look at:

- Sole owners
- Partnerships
- Private limited companies
- Cooperatives

A small business could use any of these forms of business organisation, but some firms are more suited to one particular type of organisation and some firms must be a particular type of organisation by law.

Sole owners

Many businesses start as sole owners. Klippers in Unit 2 and Fred Jones (builders) were both examples of sole owners. They are easy to set up, there are few rules governing them and they do not need to make their accounts public.

Key points about sole owners

- There is only one owner but s/he can employ as many other workers as s/he wishes.
- All of the profits go to the sole owner but s/he also bears any losses the firm makes.
- Sole owners have unlimited liability — their personal possessions are at risk if the business goes bankrupt. So this type of organisation is best suited to businesses which are unlikely to run into large amounts of debt.
- Like most small businesses, sole owners often find it difficult to raise large amounts of capital by obtaining loans.
- There is no one to share the responsibility of the business with.

exercise
1 Name any four local sole owner businesses and state what each does.
2 List the advantages and disadvantages of being a sole owner (use the case studies on pages 15–22 to assist you).
3 Interview any sole owner to find out the benefits of being a sole owner as well as the problems.

Partnerships

Many professionals, such as doctors, solicitors, accountants, etc, form themselves into partnerships. Most professions are not allowed by law to be limited companies and they often involve little capital. There is nothing, of course, to stop businesses other than the professions from forming themselves into partnerships.

Key points about partnerships

- Partnerships are owned by between two and twenty partners (in some cases more partners are allowed).
- Partnerships can employ as many people as they wish.
- Most partnerships have unlimited liability.
- If one partner leaves the partnership, or dies, then the whole partnership comes to an end.
- A decision made by one partner is binding on all the other partners.
- Partnerships are easy and cheap to set up.
- Partnerships normally draw up a document called the *Deed of Partnership*: this sets out the details of the partnership, such as
  how the profits are going to be shared out,
  how much holiday each partner is allowed,
  how much capital each partner is putting into the business.

DEED OF PARTNERSHIP

Between: Jane Peters
    and: Richard Kelly

Capital : Each partner will contribute initial capital to the value of £10,000.

Profits : Profits will be shared equally.

(*Note.* It is possible for a person to invest capital in a partnership and have limited liability. This partner is known as a 'sleeping partner'. For example if a sleeping partner invested £5000 in a partnership and it went bankrupt owing £50,000, the sleeping partner would only lose a maximum of £5000 — the other partners would be required to pay the remaining sum of money owed.)

Peters and Kelly Medical Practitioners

Jane Peters and Richard Kelly qualified as doctors five years ago. They have both been working in other practices in order to gain experience but recently decided to set up their own practice together. They felt it was a good idea to work together because they could put their money together to rent premises, they could use the same receptionist and they could cover for each other when either of them was away from the practice for any reason. They could also take turns in being on duty for emergency calls at night or at the weekend.

They contacted a solicitor and she advised them to become a partnership.

She drew up a deed of partnership for them which stated:
exactly what each was contributing to the business,
how much salary each was entitled to,
how their bills were to be paid,
what holidays each could take,
and several other details. They paid the solicitor a small sum of money for drawing up the document which was done very quickly and simply.

If the practice does well in the future it is possible that Jane and Richard will take on more partners or possibly employ newly qualified doctors who will not be made partners immediately.

questions

1 What advantages were there for Jane and Richard in combining to form a practice? (Can you think of any other advantages apart from those mentioned in the passage?)

2 Jane and Richard were good friends, so why do you think they were advised to set their practice up as a partnership with a legal document when they could have just agreed between themselves?

3 Apart from those things mentioned in the passage, what other details do you think they should have included in their deed of partnership?

4 Why do you think that Jane and Richard may wish to take on more partners in the future even though this will mean more people sharing in the profits of the practice?

exercise

Try to find five examples of partnerships in your local area. Check each one carefully to make sure it is still a partnership, and briefly state what it does.

Private Limited Companies

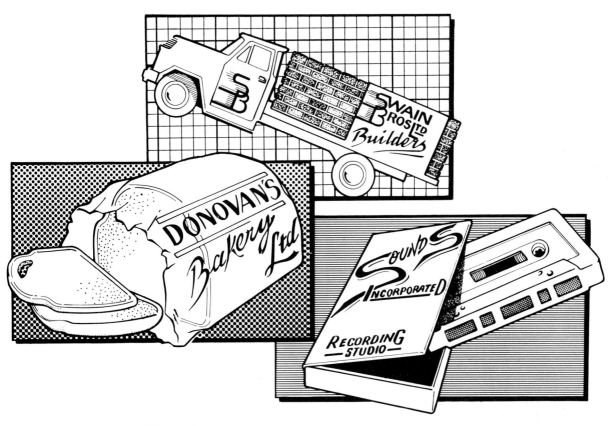

Key points

- A private limited company can be set up by a minimum of two people (there is no maximum).
- The owners of a company are known as the shareholders — they each hold at least one share in the company.
- Each owner has limited liability: if the company goes bankrupt, they can only lose the value of their shares. Personal property is not at risk.
- The owners appoint directors to run the company. The owners may or may not take part in the actual running of the company.
- The company is separate from its owners, for example the company can sue and be sued.
- Each year the company must hold a general meeting of shareholders.
- Each year, shareholders must be sent a copy of the accounts and these must also be sent to the Registrar of Companies (see page 34) where they can be viewed by anyone.
- Shares cannot be sold to the general public on the Stock Exchange and they cannot be transferred to other people without the permission of the directors.
- Private limited companies have *Ltd* (Limited) after their name. This distinguishes them from Public Limited Companies which are identified by having PLC after their name.

case study

Setting up a limited company: JJ's Disco

Scene Meeting between Julie Jason, sole owner of the successful JJ's Disco, and her accountant, Sally Watson.

Sally: So you're thinking about expanding JJ's and setting up elsewhere?

Julie: Yes, JJ's is going so well and there does seem to be the need for another one — I was thinking about using that old warehouse near the station in Castlebury.

Sally: Sounds like a good idea to me — perhaps I can give you some advice now you are heading for the big time. Have you thought about setting up a limited company?

Julie: Isn't that a bit complicated and expensive?

Sally: Not really. I can do the paper work and you can buy a ready-made company off the shelf for as little as £50 — or a bit more if you want to set up your own one.

Julie: Wouldn't it involve me in a lot of red tape? Keeping proper accounts and records. You know I've never been very good at that sort of thing!

Sally: Well, you do need to send a copy of your accounts each year to the Registrar of Companies. They keep a check on you to make sure you are operating your business properly. But don't worry, I'll handle your accounts for you. For a fee, of course!

Julie: All this is going to cost me money. What's in it for me?

Sally: For a start, you and any other owners will each have limited liability. That means that only the business is at risk. If you get into debt, you can't lose your personal possessions. You can invite other people to become shareholders in your business and raise more capital. Banks may also be keener to give you a loan and there may be some tax savings too.

Julie: I can't form a company by myself, can I?

Sally: No, but you only need one other person to join you and you can have as many shareholders as you wish.

Julie: Why would anyone else want to be a shareholder in my business?

Sally: Well, they know how successful you've been already, and by becoming shareholders they would expect a share in the profits of the business. They're not going to invest money in your business for nothing.

Julie: What if I don't make any profits?

Sally: Then your shareholders won't get any dividend on their shares — that's a risk they take. But remember they can only lose the value of their shares if the worst happened and you went bankrupt.

Julie: Well, it's certainly worth thinking about. Can I let you know in a few days time?

exercise

What would you do in Julie's position? Draw up two tables, one giving the advantages of becoming a private limited company, the other giving the disadvantages. Based on the evidence from your tables, make a decision and explain your thinking.

Julie forms a limited company

Julie decided to take Sally's advice and asked her to set up JJ's as a limited company. Julie invited her friend Tracey to join her as a director. These are the steps that Sally took to set the company up;

```
                                                    ┌──────────────────┐
                                                    │              4   │
                                                    │  JJ's Disco Ltd  │
                                                    │  formed.         │
                                                    └──────────────────┘
┌─────────────────────────────┐  ┌──────────────────┐  ┌──────────────┐  ┌───────────┐
│ Legal Documents          1  │  │              2   │  │ Certificate of 3│ │ Shares 5  │
│ called Memorandum of        │→ │ Registrar of     │→ │ Incorporation.  │ │ Sold.     │
│ Association                  │  │ Companies.       │  │              │  │           │
│ & Articles of Association.   │  └──────────────────┘  └──────────────┘  └───────────┘
│ Drawn up by Sally and Julie.│
└─────────────────────────────┘
```

The Memorandum of Association states:

- The name of the business.
- The type of business it is engaged in.
- The names of one director and the company secretary.
- The address where the company is registered.
- How much share capital it intends to raise.
- It also guarantees the limited liability of all its shareholders.

exercise

Assignment For the business you thought of in Unit 2 (page 15), draw up your own Memorandum of Association based on the one for JJ's.

The Articles of Association

- These refer to: The internal running of the company.
- The powers of the managing director.
- Procedures to be followed at meetings, salaries of directors, etc.

The Certificate of Incorporation

This is issued once the Registrar of Companies is satisfied with all the details. This gives the company permission to start trading.

```
Memorandum of          (The Companies
Association            Act 1948, 1976
of                     & 1981)
JJ's Disco Ltd

1. The name of the company is:
   JJ's Disco Ltd.

2. The registered office of the company
   is: 18 Elm Grove, Peddlescombe, West
   Yorkshire, England.

3. The objects for which the company is
   established are: to run discotheques
   and other forms of public entertainment
   in the UK.

4. The liability of members is limited.

5. The share capital of the company is
   £5000 divided into 5000 shares of £1
   each.

Names, Addresses and Descriptions of
Subscribers:
                            Number of
                            Shares

Julie Jason
18 Elm Grove                One
Peddlescombe
West Yorkshire
Company Director

Tracey Smith
20 The Vale                 One
Castlebury
West Yorkshire
Company Director
```

Shares

Julie invited a number of friends and relatives to become shareholders in JJ's Disco Ltd. The shares were sold at £1 each and Julie issued share certificates to everyone who agreed to become a part owner in her company.

No.   SHARES

J.J.'s DISCO   **LIMITED**
INCORPORATED UNDER THE COMPANIES ACTS OF 1948   1976   1981

CAPITAL   £5000

DIVIDED INTO 5000   **SHARES OF** £1   **EACH**

This is to certify that   PAUL RICHARD JONES
of   19 Western Road, Peddlescombe, West Yorkshire
is the holder of   ONE HUNDRED   Shares fully paid
of   each Numbered   251   to   350   inclusive in
the above named Company subject to the Memorandum
and Articles of Association thereof.
Given under the Common Seal of the said Company.

the   3rd day of   JULY   1987

              Julie Jason
              Tracey Smith   DIRECTORS

              Peter Parker   SECRETARY

NO TRANSFER OF THE WHOLE OR ANY PORTION OF THE ABOVE SHARES CAN BE REGISTERED WITHOUT THE PRODUCTION OF THIS CERTIFICATE

assignment   Draw up a share certificate for your company and make it out to anyone who has agreed to become a shareholder.

Explain what the possible benefits are of being a shareholder in your business as well as the possible risks involved.

Cooperatives

Cooperatives have become increasingly common as a form of business organisation in the UK. Many new businesses have been set up as cooperatives and in some cases existing businesses have been bought out by the workers to form a cooperative. Cooperatives have been encouraged as a way of helping to reduce the problem of unemployment — especially in inner city areas.

Key points about cooperatives

- The workers are all owners in the firm,
  share in the profits of the business,
  make decisions on the running of the business.
- Cooperatives may be registered as limited companies or they may be registered under the *Industrial and Provident Societies Act.*
- There are various forms of cooperatives. Workers are normally paid a salary by the firm as well as sharing in the profits of the business.
- Help and advice can be provided in the form of a *Cooperative Development Agency* (CDAs)
- There is no limit to the number of members in a cooperative.

Midland Gazette

Management and Worker buy out at Haplows

It was confirmed yesterday evening that management and workers are buying the bankrupt Haplows Brewery from the existing owner. The new business will be known as 'Haplows Cooperative Brewery'. "We decided to keep the old name because customers know and appreciate our products" said Sid Wright, the new managing director.

Most of the workers at the old Haplows Brewery have bought into the new cooperative. Asked whether he felt that the new cooperative would be more successful than the old brewery Sid Wright commented, "We are working for ourselves now, we have to make a go of it. Industrial relations at Haplows have not been good in recent times. There were two really damaging disputes in the last year alone. That's one thing that should improve now that we are all working together."

But Jim Longford, managing director of local rivals, Knutfords Brewery, questioned whether the new cooperative would have the necessary financial, technical and management skills to turn Haplows into a profit-making business. Another major problem, he thought, could well be a lack of capital . . .

case study questions

1 Give two reasons why the new cooperative might be more successful than the old Haplows Brewery.
2 Why might the new cooperative lack the 'necessary financial, technical and management skills'?
3 What benefits might there be for the workers in the new cooperative?
4 What disadvantages might there be for the workers in the new cooperative?
5 Why might there be a lack of capital in the new cooperative?

Summary of key words and ideas

- Limited liability — only the assets of the business are at risk
- Unlimited liability — the owner's personal possessions are at risk in the business in the case of bankruptcy.
- Assets — the value of the business, the buildings, machinery, stock etc.
- Receiver — person called in to distribute the assets of the business to those people owed money.
- A limited liability company may not be able to settle all its debts even after all its assets are sold.
- Businesses which are likely to incur large debts normally become limited companies.
- Some professions are not allowed limited liability and many adopt the partnership as the form of business organisation.
- Deed of partnership — a legal agreement between the partners setting out how the partnership is to be operated.
- Memorandum of Association — a legal document required for limited liability companies sets out the name, purpose, amount of shares of the company.
- Articles of Association — also required by Limited Liability Companies sets out the rules by which the company will be run.
- Registrar of Companies — Government agency which approves new companies and keeps company records.
- Certificate of Incorporation — document giving companies the right to start trading.
- Shareholders — owners of a company
- Dividend — interest paid on shares

Test questions on business organisation

1 Match the following businesses to a suitable form of business organisation:

a	Peter Smith, self-employed window cleaner	Private limited company
b	Hornby, Watts and Peters, Solicitors	Cooperative
c	Barkers, Wholesalers Ltd.	Sole owner
d	BRS Cycles — a firm where all the workers are owners.	Partnership

2 When you leave school, you are going to set up your own business. State what the business is, what form of business organisation you will use (sole trader, partnership, limited company, or cooperative) and give four reasons for your choice.

3 Jane Parks is currently a sole owner business making hand-made glass products. Suggest two reasons why she might want to become a limited company.

4 You are a shareholder in a limited liability company which has recently gone bankrupt owing large sums of money to its suppliers.

a What is a shareholder?

b What is meant by a company 'going bankrupt'?

c What is the most that you can lose as a shareholder?

5 You are a worker at DRB Engineering Ltd. It is announced that the owners are selling the company. A group of your fellow workers suggest buying the company and making it a workers' cooperative.

a How is a workers' cooperative different from other forms of business organisation?

b Give one argument in favour and one argument against becoming part of a possible workers' cooperative.

6 'Despite the advantages enjoyed by limited companies, many businesses prefer to remain as sole owners' Why do you think this is the case?

7 Karen is currently a sole owner fashion designer. She wants to form a partnership with her friend Nicki.

a Give two reasons why this might be a good idea.

b Explain briefly how Karen would go about becoming a partnership.

Three years later Karen and Nicki are doing very well and want to form a limited company.

c What would be the advantages of doing this?

d Explain briefly how they would go about doing this.

e They invite you as a friend but with no previous experience of the fashion business to become a shareholder in their new company. What benefits might you get from being a shareholder in their company?

Suggestions for coursework

1 Carry out a survey of businesses in your local area. List them under the headings sole owner, partnerships, limited companies, cooperatives.

a Add up the number of each type of business organisation

b Calculate each of these as a percentage of the total.

c Can you make any conclusions as to which businesses use which types of business organisation?

2 Make a study of one local private limited company. Try to find out:

a Who the main officers of the company are (Managing Director, Company Secretary, etc.

b The number of shares and the number of shareholders.

c What accounts they need to keep.

d Whether they made a profit last year and how much dividend they paid on their shares.

3 Invent a private limited company. Draw up brief memorandum and articles of association. Decide upon the amount of share capital you are going to issue and draw up a share for your company. Produce an agenda for your first general meeting of shareholders.

Unit 4   Costs, revenues and profits

aims

At the end of this unit you should understand:

▶ The difference between cost and price.
▶ The idea of fixed and variable costs.
▶ What is meant by revenue, profit and loss.
▶ The idea of a break-even point.
▶ How costs and revenues vary with output and sales.
▶ The difference between gross and net profit in business.
▶ The idea of average and marginal costs and revenues.
▶ How firms may attempt to increase profits.

Cost and price

In everyday language you might say that the shirt 'costs £12' in the sale. In business language you would say that 'the price is £12'. Costs in business means the cost of making the shirt.

Profit

LJB Textiles made £2 profit on each shirt it sold to the shop, Double Dee. It cost them £8 to make the shirt and they sold it to the shop at £10. *Profit* is the difference between *price* and *cost*.

1 What is the cost to the shop of each shirt it buys from LJB Textiles? What price does it charge to the customer?
2 How much profit does the shop make on each shirt in the example? (Give your answer both in £s and as a % of the price the shop purchases them at.)
3 How much profit will the shop make in total if it sells 100 shirts in a week (assuming the same price and cost)?
(*Note*   This would be called 'Gross Profit' as it does not take account of other costs to the shop, such as rent, wages, etc. See extension section on page 40 for a fuller explanation.)

Fixed and variable costs

Look again at LJB's costs of producing a shirt. We can divide these costs into two types: *fixed* and *variable*. Fixed costs remain the same regardless of how many are produced. (Rent is a fixed cost — the same amount needs to be paid out each week whether LJB produces 10 shirts or 1000). LJB will need to pay fixed costs even when the factory is closed for holidays. Variable costs are those costs which increase with the amount produced (the cost of materials, for example, will rise as LJB produce more shirts).

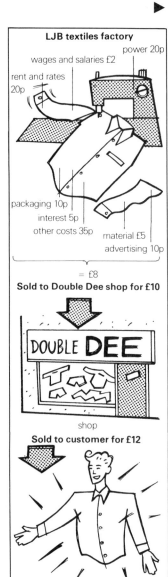

LJB textiles factory

power 20p
wages and salaries £2
rent and rates 20p
packaging 10p
interest 5p
other costs 35p
material £5
advertising 10p

= £8
Sold to Double Dee shop for £10

DOUBLE **DEE**

shop

Sold to customer for £12

customer

The cost of producing a shirt

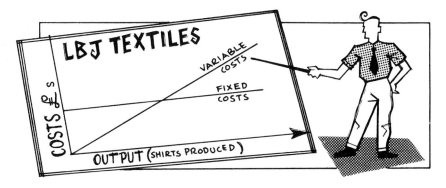

Total costs

> Total Costs = Fixed Costs *plus* Variable Costs.

Average costs

Average costs are total costs divided by the number of things produced. The example given of LJB shows an average cost of £8 per shirt.

exercise Take LJB's costs and divide them into fixed and variable costs, depending on whether you think they would stay the same or increase as they produced more.

> Some costs may be either fixed or variable, depending upon the length of time under consideration. In the short term, for example, the number of workers we employ may be fixed, so that we might regard wages as a fixed cost. In the long term, however, we might take on more workers, so wages become a variable cost.
>
> In the very long term, all costs may be regarded as being variable. A firm might use a second factory, for example, and thus increase its rent.

exercise 1 Complete the following table for LJB Textiles assuming that its fixed costs are £2000 each week and its variable costs are £6 for each shirt produced.

LJB Textiles production costs per week									
Shirts produced	0	100	200	300	400	500	600	700	800
Fixed costs (£)									
Variable costs (£)									
Total costs (£)									

2 Draw a line graph to show the information in the table. Use a different colour for fixed costs, variable costs and total costs.

Revenue
This is the amount of money a firm gets from selling a good or service.
It is found by taking the price of the item and multiplying it by the
number of units sold. If LJB Textiles sell 100 shirts to the shop Double
Dee at £10 each, its revenue will be £1000

exercise

1 Complete the following table for LJB Textiles assuming that each
shirt is sold to the shops at £10.

Revenue from the sale of shirts

Number of shirts sold per week	0	100	200	300	400	500	600	700	800
Revenue (£)									

2 Using the information from your costs graph, show total costs on a
graph similar to the one shown here.

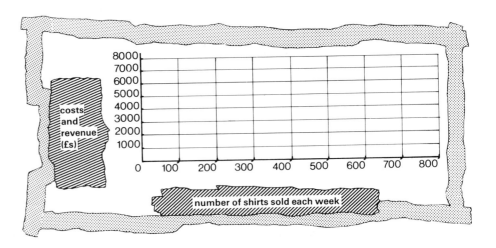

Now mark on the graph your revenue figures from the table above using
a different colour.

*A reminder about profit. We saw earlier that profit is the difference
between what it costs to produce something and what it is sold for. Another
way of saying this is that profit is the difference between total cost and total
revenue.*

LJB increases profit

3 Look at your graph showing total cost and total revenue again. Find
the point where the revenue and cost lines cross. This is known as the
break-even point. How much is being produced here? How much
profit is made here? Why do you think that this is called the break-
even point? Would LJB Textiles go bankrupt if it continued to
produce at the break-even point?

Losses at LJB

Loss

A loss is made if a firm sells its goods or services for less than it costs to make them. In other words, it makes a loss when total cost is greater than total revenue.

4 Using your graph, complete the following table:

Number of shirts made and sold per week	0	100	200	300	400	500	600	700	800
Profit (+) Loss(-) (£)									

extension section

Average and marginal costs and revenues

We have seen already that average costs are found by taking total costs and dividing them by the number of units produced. Average revenue is found by taking total revenue and dividing by the number of items sold. If price does not vary, then average revenue will be the same as the price. (Because revenue is *price × number of units sold*)

Marginal cost is the cost of producing one extra item. For example if 100 shirts cost £800 to make and 101 shirts cost £807 we say that the marginal cost of the 101st shirt is £7 (£807–£800). Because fixed costs do not vary with production, the marginal cost will be equal to the variable cost of producing an extra unit.

Marginal revenue is the revenue gained from selling one more unit of a product or service. For example, revenue from sale of 100 shirts = £1200, revenue from 101 shirts = £1212. The marginal revenue from the sale of the 101st shirt = £12 (£1212 − £1200). If the price does not change with sales then the marginal revenue will be the same as price (because the addition to revenue of selling one extra item will be the same each time).

extension exercise

1 Complete the following table of LJB Textiles production and sale of T-shirts per week

No. produced and sold	1000	1001	1002	1003	1004	1005
Total cost (£s)	2800	2802	2804	2805	2806	2807
Marginal cost (£s)	—	2	?	?	?	?
Total revenue (£s)	3000	3003	3006	3009	3012	3015
Marginal revenue (£s)	—	3	?	?	?	?

2 What is the average cost of producing 1000 units?

3 What price was charged when 1000 units were sold?

4 Where was the largest profit made and how much was it?

Gross and net profit

A distinction is sometimes made in business between profits made before *overheads*, such as rent, rates and interest, have been paid and profits after all expenses have been paid out. Profits before overhead payments have been made are called *gross profits*, and *net profits* are what is left when all costs have been met. You will see that in our examples we have used net profit in the case of LJB Textiles and gross profit in the case of the shop Double Dee. Net profit is what is available to the owners of the firm to use as they wish.

DOUBLE DEE SHOP	Gross Profit = Selling Price less Buying Price ($12 − $10 = $2)	→	Net Profit = Gross Profit ($2) less Costs ($1·50) (wages, rent, lighting, etc.) ($2 − $1·50 = 50p)

Do profits mean success?

Profits are certainly one guide to how successful a firm is, but we must remember that profits are only one aim of the firm and in some cases they may not be an aim at all. Many small businessmen are often happy just to survive in business and to make a reasonable living. Making larger profits may mean a great deal more hard work and responsibility. Some organisations, such as clubs, charities and state-owned businesses may exist in order to provide a service rather than to make a profit.

Do large profits mean that a firm is efficient?

Not necessarily — a firm may be very good at producing something, but because of a great deal of competition it may not be able to charge a price high enough to make large profits. On the other hand, a firm may be able to charge very high prices for something and make large profits without being very efficient.

1 Name a good or service where there is a great deal of competition (ie there are a large number of different producers).
2 Name a good or service where there is very little competition (ie there are very few different producers).
3 Name two non-profit-making organisations.

Profit as a percentage of turnover

Even if we take profits as a guide to success, total profits by themselves mean very little — large firms would be expected to make bigger profits than small firms. A better guide is to look at profits as a % of revenue (sometimes referred to as *turnover*). This gives us an idea of what our *return* is on sales.

For example, the shop Double Dee pays £2000 for 200 shirts and sells them for £2400. Its gross profit is therefore £400. Its % profit is calculated as
£400/£2400 × 100 = 16.6%.
Remember, out of this, Double Dee would also have to pay its overhead expenses, so this might not be a very good return on its sales.

1 Calculate LJB's net profit as a % of sales from the table you constructed when it makes and sells, **a** 100 shirts, **b** 500 shirts. What does this tell you about LJB's performance?

Increasing the profit. Remember, profit is the difference between revenue and costs — so if we want to try and increase profits we can either try and increase revenue or reduce costs.

2 As accountant for LJB Textiles you are given the following figures:

	1984	1985	1986	1987
Sales Revenue (£000)	50	65	80	85
Total Net profit (£000)	10	12	14	15

a Calculate LJB's profit as % of sales.
b What comments would you make about LJB's performance 1984–1987?
c What advice would you give to LJB Textiles to help them increase their profits? (For example, change prices, advertise more, reduce the workforce, use better machines, improve the product, etc.) Explain how you would expect your ideas to work in terms of either reducing costs or increasing revenue.

Summary of key words and ideas

- *Costs* are how much it costs to make a product or supply a service.
- *Price* is what the supplier charges for a product or service.
- *Fixed costs* are those costs which do not vary with the amount produced.
- *Variable costs* rise as the amount produced increases.
- *Revenue* is the amount obtained from selling a good or service.
- *Profit* is the difference between revenue and costs (net profit takes account of all costs, gross profit simply looks at the difference between the buying and selling price of goods and does not take account of other costs).
- *Break-even point* is where a firm's revenue is equal to its costs and its net profit will be zero.
- *Losses* occur if costs exceed revenue.
- To increase profits a firm must either try and increase its revenue (by advertising, changing prices, improving the product, etc.) or reduce its costs (by being more efficient, using better machinery, getting cheaper supplies, etc.)
- *Profits as a % of revenue* (turnover) is one measure of the success of a firm.
- Some firms may have aims other than making the largest possible profits.
- Average cost = total costs/number of units produced.
- Average revenue = total revenue/number of units sold.
- Marginal cost = cost of producing one extra unit.
- Marginal revenue = revenue gained from selling one extra unit.

Suggestions for coursework

1 Invent a small manufacturing firm. Make two lists — one for fixed costs, one for variable costs. Try and put actual values to these costs. Decide on a selling price for your product. Show on a graph costs and revenues and mark clearly the break-even point. Suggest ways in which you might try and go about increasing profits in the future.

2 For a real life small business (for example a shop) try and find out the approximate running costs (the fixed costs) and the cost of goods bought each month. Try and work out net and gross profit, and the break-even point.

3 Interview owners of small businesses to try and find out what their aims are (do they try and make the largest possible profits, or sell as much as possible, or try and survive, or what?)

4 Look at the costs and revenues involved in the running of a school or college function, such as a disco or a play. What is the break-even point? How are prices established? Why are prices not higher/lower?

Test questions on costs, revenues and profits

Read the following passage carefully and then answer the questions which follow:

John Stevens runs a greengrocer's business in a small village. Every morning he gets up very early and drives his van to the main town to buy fruit and vegetables at the wholesale market. At busy times of the year John employs a lad to help him. John does not own the shop but pays rent each week to a landlord. In addition to this, John has to pay for any lighting and heating he uses.

1 Make a list of all the costs mentioned in the passage that John pays out for each week.

2 Put a letter F next to any cost which is fixed (ie those costs which John has to pay for no matter how much he sells) and a letter V against those costs which vary with the amount he sells.

3 Name three other costs not mentioned in the passage which John might need to meet in his business. In each case say whether they are fixed or variable.

4 Last week John sold 50 lbs of tomatoes at 40 pence per pound. What was his revenue on tomatoes?

5 If John increased the price of his tomatoes to 50 pence a pound, do you think his revenue would go up, down or remain the same — explain your answer. (There is no one correct answer to this question.)

6 Explain how John would go about calculating his 'take-home' profit each month.

7 Last week John bought 100 lbs of apples at 20 pence per pound. He sold the first 50 lbs at 40 pence and then reduced the price to 30 pence for the remaining 50 lbs.
   a What was his total revenue on apples?
   b What was his gross profit on apples?
   c What was his gross profit as a % of turnover on apples?
   d What was his marginal revenue on the 21st lb of apples?

8 John makes a reasonable living but he is ambitious and wants to do better. As an adviser for small businesses, suggest a plan for John in order to assist him in making larger profits in the future. Explain the various parts of your plan, saying why you feel that this would help to improve his business. Use the following statistics on John's business to assist you in deciding upon the plan:

Stevens the Greengrocers

	1985	1986	1987
Sales Revenue (£000s)	104	110	120
Gross Profit (£000s)	51	52	54
Net Profit (£000s)	10	11	12

Unit 5   Financing the small business

Aims   **At the end of this unit you should understand:**
- The need for finance.
- The difference between fixed capital and working capital.
- The types of finance available for small businesses.
- Simple business accounts.
- How a firm calculates how much finance it requires.
- The cash flow problem.

Why do we need finance?

case study   **The case of Ling's pottery**

Ling Lau wants to develop her hobby of pottery into a small business. She lives in a small market town in an area which attracts lots of tourists. There are some suitable small premises up for sale for £15 000. She will need to spend about £2000 converting these to a pottery. She has the offer of a second-hand wheel, kiln and other necessary equipment for a further £3000. She will need another £500 for clay, glazes and other materials. Then there will be the running costs of the business, such as electricity and rates, — she calculates these at about £100 a month. She has set £10 a week aside for advertising in local papers and the tourist office.

Although Ling has already made a selection of items for sale, she feels that she will need to make a bigger range of pottery before she is able to really open the business. She doesn't expect to make any sales until a month after she has set up.

Ling has managed to save up £5000. Part of this was from a redundancy payment when she lost her job at a local firm last year.

questions   1 How much money will Ling require to set up and run her business for the first month? Set the items out in a table.

2 How much capital (money) could Ling contribute to the business and how has she managed to obtain this?

Fixed capital and working capital

Some of the items Ling requires money for are things which will remain permanently in the business — the premises, for example. These items are called *fixed assets* and the money used to buy them is *fixed capital*. Ling also requires money for things which will be used up in the business, for example the clay. For these items she will need *working capital*.

exercise Make two lists, one of Ling's fixed capital and one for her working capital (include any additional items you can think of which are not mentioned.)

How can the small business raise capital?

Ling has managed to raise £5000 of capital by using her own savings and a redundancy payment from her previous job. Many small businesses get their initial capital in this way. Other people would be very reluctant to lend money to Ling if she was not prepared to make a financial commitment herself by putting some of her own money into the business.

Despite her £5000, Ling still needs a great deal more capital in order to start her business. She has heard that the government is keen to encourage people to set up small businesses. She made enquiries at a local Enterprise Centre. The Enterprise Centre was set up by the local authority to help attract businesses to the area and to encourage people to start up their own firms as a way of trying to reduce unemployment. Ling lives in an area where there is high unemployment and there are a number of special schemes available to help small businesses.

Ling found her time at the Enterprise Centre was very usefully spent. Although the Enterprise Centre did not themselves have money to loan her, they gave her a great deal of very useful advice about where to obtain finance from and how to apply for it. They also suggested that she went on a short training course at her local college to learn about the financial side of operating a small business — how to keep the books and fill in VAT returns for example. They even introduced her to someone else who was wanting to set up a pottery and suggested they might want to get together to set up the business.

Financial assistance from the government

C.O.S.I.R.A.

Loans for
small
businesses

THROUGH THE GOVERNMENT
LOAN GUARANTEE SCHEME

TYNESIDE
ENTERPRISE ZONE
GETS YOU GOING.

There is a range of different types of assistance offered by the Government to small businesses through the Training Agency (TA) and the Department of Trade and Industry. Some of these vary, depending upon the area you live in. Areas with very high levels of unemployment tend to get the greatest amount of assistance. Some areas are called *Enterprise Zones* and these get special help. Many local authorities also have their own schemes to encourage small businesses. Government and local authority help tends to change quite frequently and you need to check exactly what is available in your area.

These are some examples of the types of assistance which the Enterprise Centre suggested to Ling:

The Enterprise Allowance Scheme

As soon as Ling starts her own business she will not be allowed to claim unemployment benefit. This is a real problem for unemployed people like Ling wishing to set up businesses. Ling found out that she could apply to the TA for an Enterprise Allowance which would pay her £40 each week for a year while she tried to build her business up. Ling fulfilled all the conditions required by the TA — she was over 18, had been unemployed for more than 13 weeks and was prepared to invest at least £1000 of her own money in the business.

The Small Firms Service (SFS)

Like the Enterprise Centre, the SFS does not provide actual finance itself but it was able to provide Ling with free information and low cost financial advice. It helped her prepare an application form for a loan from her bank and put her in touch with a successful local business which could offer all sorts of practical advice.

Government guaranteed loans scheme

Ling asked at the Small Firms Service about the possibility of obtaining a loan from her local bank. They explained that banks were often reluctant to lend to new businesses before they had shown themselves to be profitable. They suggested she should apply for a loan under the Government Loan Guarantee Scheme — this means that the government agrees to repay 80% of the loan to the bank if for any reason Ling was unable to do so herself. The scheme is for loans from £5000 to £75 000 and a premium of 3% is charged by the Department of Industry for the guarantee. The bank still needs to approve the scheme before a loan is given and Ling needed help from the SFS in preparing her application for a loan.

Grants for capital equipment

The SFS told Ling that because the pottery was in an 'Assisted Area', she could apply for a Regional Development grant from the Government to help pay for part of the cost of the buildings and other fixed assets. There were also quite generous grants available from the local authority where she lived. She was again given assistance with preparing an application for these grants by the SFS. She was also told that in the first year she would pay lower rates on the business to the local authority.

COSIRA

Ling's business is located in a rural area and she was able to apply for additional help and advice from the Council for Small Industries in Rural Areas.

Small firms set up with aid from business venture schemes

How can banks help?

Ling already had a bank account and the SFS suggested that she arranged an appointment with her bank manager to discuss her ideas with him. She found this to be very useful. In the first place, the bank was prepared to offer her a great deal of very valuable advice free of charge. When it came to talking about borrowing money, the manager was able to explain to Ling the important difference between loans and overdrafts.

Loans and overdrafts

The manager explained that overdrafts are normally for short-term borrowing. They were particularly useful for *cash flow* problems when the business might temporarily run short of cash even though it had plenty of orders (see page 53).

For example, before the main holiday season Ling would have to buy materials and produce her pottery. She would hope to sell most of the pottery in the holiday season but might well need an overdraft to assist her finances until then. An overdraft would enable Ling to write out cheques for more than was in her account. In other words, she could officially overdraw on her account up to an amount agreed by her bank. She would pay interest only on the amount by which she was overdrawn and the bank had the right to withdraw the overdraft facility at any time.

The manager explained to Ling that a loan was for longer-term finance. It was a fixed sum of money to be paid back with interest over an agreed number of years and had to be used for a particular purpose in the business — normally for fixed assets, such as the purchase of the kiln.

exercise   Read through the example of Ling's Pottery and list all the possible sources of finance and assistance mentioned.

Calculating the need for finance: cash flow

extension section   Ling had managed to calculate how much she needed to set up her pottery, but what concerned her now was how to work out the amount of finance she would require once the business was running. Her bank manager was very helpful here — he showed her how to draw up a *cash flow forecast*.

This is a table estimating her income and expenditure on a monthly basis for the first six months after she sets up the pottery. The table they came up with for the first three months using the standard bank form is shown below. The *Budget* column shows the estimates and the *Actual* column will be completed by Ling at the end of each month to check on the accuracy of the forecast amounts. The bottom line indicates the size of the overdraft Ling requires each month.

Cash Flow forecast from ____ MARCH ____ 19 __87__ to ____ AUGUST ____ 19 __87__

Branch ____ LAPSFORD ____ Account ____ LING LAV ____ Business ____ LING'S POTTERY ____

Period e.g. Four weeks/Month/Quarter	MARCH		APRIL		MAY								TOTAL	
	Budget	Actual	Budget	Actual	Budget	Actual	Budget	Actual	Budget	Actual	Budget	Actual	Budget	Actual
Receipts														
Cash Sales	50		200		300									
From Debtors	0		20		40									
Other Revenue Sources	160		160		160									
TOTAL A	210		380		500									
Purchases														
Payments														
Cash Purchases	60		60		80									
To Creditors	20		40		50									
Wages/Salaries/P.A.Y.E.	160		160		160									
Rent/Rates/Insurance	30		30		30									
Light/Heat/Power	50		50		40									
Transport/Packaging														
Repairs/Renewals														
H.P. Payments/Leasing Charges	40		40		40									
Bank/Finance charge & interest	50		50		50									
Sundry Expenses	20		40		60									
TOTAL B	430		470		510									
A – B (net inflow) or B – A (net outflow) — **C** Cr or Dr	220		90		10									
Bank balance at end of previous period brought forward — **D** Cr or Dr	Cr 100 / Dr		120		210									
Bank balance at end of period carried forward *Aggregate of C and D* — Cr or Dr	120		210		220									

questions

1 Why are receipts low in the first month?
2 In which month does Ling estimate that she will require the largest overdraft?
3 Give two reasons why Ling's budget column may be different from the actual column.
4 Why would Ling expect to reduce the size of her overdraft in the future?

exercise Either continue Ling's cash flow forecast for a further three months or draw up a similar table for your own business.

Simple business accounts

Ling has now been operating her business for a year and her bank wants to see a set of simple accounts for the pottery. Accounts show how the business is doing by recording how it has spent money, its income from sales and the value of its assets.

There are various types of accounts, but in the case of a small business these could be relatively simple. Even so, Ling thought it was a good idea to get some help from a qualified accountant. She had kept careful records each week of the money she had spent and the revenue she had received from the sale of pottery. These proved to be very useful to the accountant when drawing up the accounts for the business.

The accountant drew up a *Trading, Profit and Loss Account* for Ling's Pottery. The summary of this is shown below;

Notes on the Trading, Profit and Loss Account

- Cost of goods sold is calculated by:
  Sales *less* Stock at the start of the year *plus* Purchases of materials during the year *less* Closing stock
- Gross profit is calculated by:
  Sales *less* Cost of goods sold
- Net profit is calculated by: Gross profit *less* Expenses
- *Appropriation* This section in the accounts shows how the net profit is used. In the example given, Ling has drawn out £3000 for her own use and kept £6500 in the business.

Ling did well to make a small profit in her first year of trading. She was helped by the Enterprise Allowance. In the next year of trading she will not be receiving this assistance so it will be important for her to increase her sales.

questions

1 In your business your opening stock is valued at £4000, you make purchases of materials valued at £3000 and your closing stock is £2000. Your sales for the year are £20 000. Calculate,
   a the cost of goods sold,
   b the gross profit for the year.
2 In the same business, your total expenses for the year come to £8000. Calculate the net profit.

exercise

Draw up a trading, profit and loss account for your own business. Write a brief note to someone unfamiliar with accounts, explaining what the various totals show about the business.

LING'S POTTERY

27 THE LANE, UPPER THEIKSTON,
CORNWALL, EX13 4GF
Tel: (0730) 12378

Trading Profit Loss A/c year ending 31/3/88

Trading a/c

	£		£
Opening stock	1500	Sales	14000
Purchases	1200		
Total stock	1700		
Closing stock	500		
Cost of goods sold	1200		
Gross profit	12800		

Profit/Loss a/c

Wages	2000	Gross profit	12800
Advertising	300		
Heating & lighting	600		
Sundries	400		
Net profit	9500		
	12800		12800

Appropriation

Drawings	3000	Net profit	9500
Retained profit	6500		
	9500		9500

The balance sheet

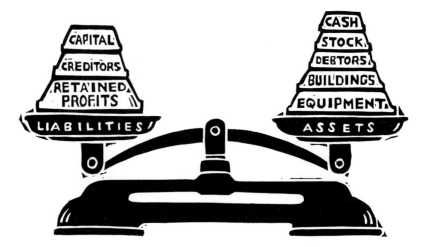

The accountant also drew up a balance sheet for Ling's business. This gives a complete picture of the business by showing on one side its *liabilities* (what the business owes) and on the other side its *assets* (what the business owns and what is due to it).

```
Balance Sheet for Ling's Pottery as at 1/3/88

LIABILITIES                        ASSETS
Capital           20000           Fixed assets
Retained profit    6500           Pottery              17000
                                  Equipment             3000
                  _____
                          26500
Current liabilities               Current assets

Creditors           500           Stock                  500
                                  Debtors                200
                                  Cash                  6300

                  _____                                _____

                  27000                                27000
```

Notes on balance sheet

- The total assets must always be equal to the total liabilities in a balance sheet.
- Creditors are people to whom the business owes money (such as for bills from suppliers not yet paid).
- Debtors are people who owe the business money (such as customer orders not yet paid for).

exercise   Draw up a balance sheet for your own business. Explain what the balance sheet shows about the current financial position of the business.

Summary of key words and ideas

- *Fixed Capital* is finance used for purchasing *Fixed Assets* — equipment which remains permanently in the business.
- *Working Capital* is finance for items which will be used up in the business, eg raw materials.
- Finance for small businesses comes from a variety of sources. These include:
  1. the owner's own savings,
  2. redundancy payments,
  3. bank loans and overdrafts,
  4. partnership capital,
  5. shares, in the case of limited companies,
  6. central government,
  7. local government,
  8. charities, (eg the Prince's Trust).
- additional finance is often available to firms in Assisted Areas where there is high unemployment.
- A *bank loan* is a fixed sum of money given for a particular purpose and paid back with interest over an agreed period of time.
- A *bank overdraft* allows the business to overspend on its account up to an agreed maximum. Interest is only charged on the amount by which the account is overdrawn. Often used for expenditure which is irregular or unexpected.
- A *cash flow problem* is when the business runs short of cash because its money is tied up in stock or other assets, including debtors (people who owe the business money).
- Creditors are people to whom the business owes money.
- The *Trading, Profit and Loss Account* of a business shows its gross and net profit or loss over a particular period of time.
- The *assets* are all those items belonging to or owed to a business.
- The *liabilities* are anything the business owes.
- The *Balance Sheet* shows all the assets and liabilities of a business at a particular date.

Suggestions for coursework

1. Set up an imaginary business. Find out as much as you can about different forms of finance available. Show how you might use these to finance different aspects of your business. Try and include information on the rates of interest that would be charged to you. Explain why you might use some forms of finance rather than others. Distinguish between fixed and working capital.
2. For any four small local businesses try and find out how they,
   a. raised their initial capital,
   b. what forms of finance they continue to use in the business,
   c. why they chose those particular forms of finance.
3. For an Assisted Area, find out about all the forms of finance available to firms wishing to set themselves up in the area. Prepare a publicity document to attract small firms to the area.

Test questions on financing the small business

1 John Jenkins owns a small garage which sells petrol and carries out repairs. John is the only owner at present. John is interested in selling his business and buying a larger garage which has recently become available. The new business would cost £100 000. John has calculated that his fixed assets are worth £40 000 and his current assets are worth £20 000. He is paying back a bank loan of £20 000 and he has reached the limit of his overdraft facility of £10 000. His bank manager is not willing to increase his loans at the current time. He is currently owed £2000 by customers.

   a How much extra finance does John require to purchase the new business?

   b What type of business organisation is John's garage?

   c Describe two ways in which John might be able to raise extra finance.

   d What is the difference between fixed assets and current assets?

   e Give an example of a fixed asset and an example of a current asset that John is likely to have in his business.

   f Explain the difference between a bank loan and an overdraft, giving an example of how John might use each in his business.

   g Using the information given above, draw up a simple balance sheet for John's garage

2 Marcia Jones is considering setting up a firm specialising in knitwear in her home town of Newcastle-upon-Tyne. She has been unemployed for the last six months but has £5000 in savings and redundancy payments.

   a Describe three ways in which Marcia could get financial help from the Government bearing in mind that Newcastle upon Tyne is in an Assisted Area.

   b Describe two ways in which Marcia's bank could assist her financially.

3 Steve Bailey Cycles Ltd. is a small manufacturer of specialised racing bikes. They have been doing well and have plenty of new orders but their accountant has told them they are facing a 'cash flow problem'.

   a What is meant by a 'cash flow problem'?

   b How might this have come about in the case of Steve Bailey Cycles Ltd.?

   c How might Steve Bailey Cycles Ltd. try and overcome their cash flow problem?

4 a What would be regarded as the fixed assets and the current assets of the firm shown in the picture opposite?

   b What types of finance might the business use for each set of assets?

55

Unit 6   Obtaining equipment and supplies

aims   At the end of this unit you should understand:

▶ How firms purchase or rent materials and equipment.
▶ The use of business documents when purchasing goods.
▶ The documents involved in purchasing from overseas.
▶ The purpose and methods of stock control.

Methods of obtaining goods and equipment

There are four main ways open to the small business wishing to obtain goods and equipment:

Cash (including cheques)

1 This is the most straightforward method of purchasing. In some cases this may be the only method available to the small business because the seller does not offer any alternative. Some sellers may require cash with the order whilst others may accept *cash on delivery* (COD). It is to the advantage of the seller to be paid immediately because s/he then has the use of the money. In order to encourage buyers to pay quickly, the seller may offer a *cash discount* — this is a certain percentage reduction in the selling price given for prompt payment.

Credit

2 If goods are bought on credit it means that the purchaser is given a certain period of time to pay for the goods after receiving them. It is quite common in business for firms to be allowed several weeks to pay for goods.

Sometimes the seller will allow credit without making any extra charge: this is known as *interest-free credit*. This is true of the supply of gas and electricity — the customer pays the bill every three months after using the gas or electricity and is not charged any extra. Sometimes the buyer will be charged interest if the goods are bought on credit. In this case the purchaser must be told,

a the cash price,
b how much interest s/he is actually paying.

Hire purchase (HP)

3 Firms sometimes buy equipment on hire purchase. This is exactly what it sounds like: the firm rents (hires) the goods whilst it is paying for the goods by instalments. The firm will normally be required to make a % down payment as a deposit on the purchase. The firm will then pay the remaining amount over a period of time by regular instalments. The items will not become the property of the firm until it has completed all the payments.

The total repayments will normally be considerably more than the cash price but the advantage to the firm is that it has the use of the equipment straight away. Hire purchase is usually arranged through a finance company which pays the seller and has the power to take back the goods from the buyer if s/he has not paid more than one third of the value of the goods.

Renting and leasing

4 In some cases firms may find it better to rent equipment rather than purchase it themselves. Firms may lack the finance to purchase the equipment or property. In other cases, they may only need to use an expensive piece of equipment very occasionally, so it does not pay them to purchase it and tie up their money unnecessarily. Another benefit of renting rather than purchasing is that usually the firm hiring the equipment is responsible for repairs and maintenance.

A special form of renting is known as *leasing*. This is when a firm rents assets over a long period of time from a leasing company. The leasing company is again responsible for maintaining and repairing the item on lease. Many firms now lease cars and other vehicles rather than purchase them. Some firms will also lease machinery and other equipment.

The Corner Shop

Ramesh Patel owns a newsagent and confectioners called The Corner Shop. Each week he purchases stock from a cash-and-carry wholesalers. The newspapers are delivered every day by a distributor and he pays for the ones he sells at the end of the month. Ramesh runs a newspaper delivery service for his customers who normally pay him each week.

The Corner Shop also offers a photocopying service. Ramesh does not own the photocopier but pays a certain amount each month to a company which maintains the machine and carries out any necessary repairs.

Ramesh has recently put a deposit down on a van and is paying instalments each month to a finance company. He uses the van to collect his stock from the wholesaler but it will not actually belong to him until he has completed paying all the instalments.

exercise

1 The Corner Shop case study gives an example of a cash purchase, leasing, hire purchase and two examples of credit. Make a list of these methods of obtaining materials and equipment and write next to each one an example of it from the Corner Shop business.

2 For each method suggest one advantage and one disadvantage of using it for Ramesh.

Ramesh is buying his van on hire purchase from Central Motors. Ramesh has signed the agreement with a finance company who have paid Central Motors. The van is second-hand and costs £4000. Ramesh was required to put a deposit of 25% down and to pay the rest in instalments. The table below shows how much he would pay at various rates of interest over different periods of time.

3 Calculate how much it will cost him on HP if he pays for the van over two years at 8% interest. (Remember, he pays a deposit first.)

4 How much more would it cost if the interest was 10% and he paid over four years?

HIRE PURCHASE REPAYMENT TABLE

FLAT RATE	6%			8%			10%			12%		
PERIOD	2 yrs	3 yrs	4 yrs	2 yrs	3 yrs	4 yrs	2 yrs	3 yrs	4 yrs	2 yrs	3 yrs	4 yrs
£50	£2.33	£1.64	£1.29	£2.42	£1.73	£1.38	£2.50	£1.81	£1.46	£2.59	£1.89	£1.55
£100	£4.67	£3.28	£2.58	£4.84	£3.45	£2.75	£5.00	£3.62	£2.92	£5.17	£3.78	£3.09
£200	£9.33	£6.56	£5.17	£9.67	£6.89	£5.50	£10.00	£7.23	£5.84	£10.34	£7.56	£6.17
£500	£23.33	£16.39	£12.92	£24.17	£17.23	£13.75	£25.00	£18.06	£14.59	£25.84	£18.89	£15.42
£600	£28.00	£19.67	£15.50	£29.00	£20.67	£16.50	£30.00	£21.67	£17.50	£31.00	£22.67	£18.50
£800	£37.33	£26.22	£20.67	£38.67	£27.56	£22.00	£40.00	£28.89	£23.34	£41.34	£30.23	£24.67
£1000	£46.67	£32.78	£25.83	£48.34	£34.45	£27.50	£50.00	£36.12	£29.17	£51.67	£37.78	£30.84
£2000	£93.34	£65.56	£51.66	£96.68	£68.90	£55.00	£100.00	£72.24	£58.34	£103.34	£75.56	£61.68
£3000	£140.01	£98.34	£77.49	£145.02	£103.35	£82.50	£150.00	£108.36	£87.51	£155.01	£113.34	£92.52
£4000	£186.68	£131.12	£103.32	£193.36	£137.80	£110.00	£200.00	£144.48	£116.68	£206.68	£151.12	£123.36
£5000	£233.35	£163.90	£129.15	£241.70	£172.25	£137.50	£250.00	£180.60	£145.85	£258.35	£188.90	£154.20

(SUM BORROWED)

Documents used in purchasing

When goods are purchased by a firm, certain documents pass between the buyer and the supplier. The most important of these are the *order form*, the *delivery note*, the *invoice, receipts, credit and debit notes* and *monthly statements*. A firm may not use all of these, but the following example of The Village Stores illustrates the purpose of each document.

case study

The Village Stores

Sally Johnston is the owner of The Village Stores, a general grocers in the village of Lastwaite. She obtains her stock from a wholesaler in Carlisle who makes a delivery each week to Lastwaite.

The order

1 Sally has a price list and details of the stock available from Carlisle Wholesalers. Each week she completes an order form and sends it to the wholesaler to let them know her requirements for the following week. This is done on a computerised form which uses code numbers for the various goods which Sally is ordering.

   Carlisle Wholesalers process the order form from The Village Stores and pack the goods ready for delivery the following week.

The delivery note

2 Carlisle Wholesalers deliver the goods to The Village Stores. The driver gives Sally a delivery note which lists all the items being delivered and shows any items unavailable. Sally checks this off against her own copy of the order.

ORDER FORM

Order No .....312.....
Date ....30/5/87.......

.... CARLISLE WHOLESALERS ....

.... CARLISLE ....

.... CUMBRIA ....

Please supply .... THE VILLAGE STORE .... (Name and Address
.... LASTWAITE .... of BUYER)
.... CUMBRIA ....

with the following goods   Ref: **VS/L.**

Quantity	Description of Goods (Please quote Stock Number)	Unit Price £	Total Value £
4 DOZ	032172 BAKED BEANS	0.15	7.20
5 DOZ	032189 TOMATOES	0.14	8.40

Del. Note No. .....499...... Order No. ....312.....

DELIVERY NOTE

.... CARLISLE WHOLESALERS ....

.... CARLISLE ....

.... CUMBRIA ....

Date 7/6 .... 19 87

Goods supplied to

.... THE VILLAGE STORE .... (Name and
.... LASTWAITE .... Address of
.... CUMBRIA .... Buyer)

Our ref: .....CW/396.... Your ref: ......VS/L......

Quantity	Description of Goods
4 DOZ	032172 BAKED BEANS
5 DOZ	032189 TOMATOES

Date .... Signed ....

The invoice

3 Carlisle Wholesalers send an invoice to The Village Stores. This is also done on a computer. The invoice gives all the details of the goods ordered and delivered including the quantity and the price. The invoice also shows any VAT being charged by the wholesaler and any discounts being allowed.

You may also find some of these terms on invoices:
Carr. paid means that the cost of the transport is already included in the price of the goods
Carr. fwd means that the buyer must pay for the transport
FOR = free on rail
FOB = free on board ship
E & O E = errors and omissions excepted. This allows the seller the right to correct any errors at a later date.
Terms These are the various discounts allowed; trade discount for recognised traders, cash discount for immediate payment in cash, seven days $2\frac{1}{2}\%$ for bills settled within a week.

Credit and debit notes

4 Carlisle Wholesalers will send the Village Stores a credit note for any amount that it may have overcharged Sally on the invoice or for damaged stock returned. A debit note is sent if Sally has been undercharged.

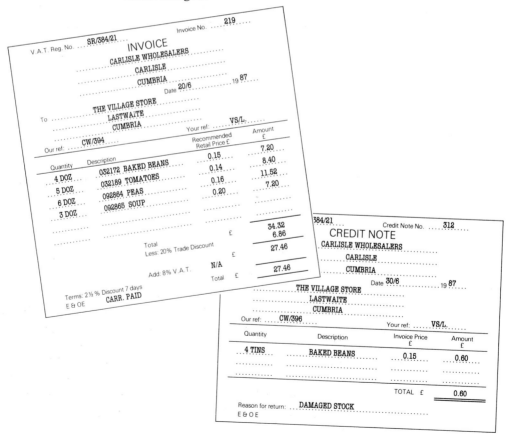

60

Monthly statements

5 Each month Carlisle Wholesalers sends Sally a statement of how much is currently owed. This lists all the invoices she has been sent and records any payment made by Sally since the last statement. The statement will also show any credit and debit notes that may have been issued during the previous month.

Receipts

6 Sally pays her bill to Carlisle Wholesalers each month and they send her a receipt to show that payment has been made.

STATEMENT OF ACCOUNT

V.A.T. Reg. No. .....SR/384/21..... 　　　　　　　　　　　　　Statement No. .....28/87.....

.... CARLISLE WHOLESALERS ....
.... CARLISLE ....
.... CUMBRIA ....

Date 31/6 .... 19 87
(the last day of the month)

To .... THE VILLAGE STORE ....
.... LASTWAITE ....
.... CUMBRIA ....

Date	Details		Debits £	Credits £	Balance £
	Balance	b/f			28.61
13/6/87	CHEQUE			6.51	22.10
20/6/87	INVOICE NO. 219		27.46		49.56
25/6/87	CHEQUE			10.16	39.40
28/6/87	CREDIT NOTE 312			0.60	38.80

Terms: Cash Discount 2½ % 7 Days 　　　　　　　　　The last amount is the amount due.

E & EO

---

exercise 1 You are the owner of Sweetway — a small confectioners which buys from CRT Wholesalers Ltd. This week you order the following items: 2 boxes of Mars Bars at £8.50 a box, 3 boxes of Bounty Bars at £8.30 a box, 5 boxes of plain crisps, 4 boxes of salt and vinegar crisps and 3 boxes of beef flavour crisps — all at £5.20 a box.

a Prepare an order form and an invoice for the items shown above.

b It is later discovered that the price charged on Mars Bars should have been £8.10 a box. Prepare an appropriate document to correct the error on the invoice.

Buying from overseas

Even quite small firms frequently need to purchase stock from overseas. In many cases they will do this through a specialist importing agency. The importing agent will arrange the documentation and the finance for the transfer of the goods. The agent will charge a percentage of the value of the goods as commission.

A firm may choose to import direct without using an agency. The firm exporting the goods will normally require payment in their own currency. The firm will probably enlist the assistance of its bank in arranging the finance. A *bill of exchange* may be drawn up by the firm exporting the goods — this guarantees that they will be paid when the goods arrive at their destination.

Another document used in international trading is the *bill of lading*. This gives the *title*, or ownership, of the goods. For example, it will be given to the shipping line at the time of loading. The bill of lading will be handed over to the firm purchasing the goods on presentation of the correct documents. The *air waybill* is a similar document used for air freight.

BILL OF LADING

SHIPPER		CARRIER CODE No 1085	YES	VOY	SHIPMENT No	CAP		TT
OUP OXFORD	A. C No	E C I AGENTS A. C No	CM AGENT		REV			
CONSIGNEE		DANGEROUS GOODS CLASSIFICATION						
N.Y. BOOKS NEW YORK U.S.A.	A. C No	TEMPERATURE CONTROL IN CENTIGRADE INSTRUCTIONS			TO			
NOTIFY ADDRESS-WITHOUT LIABILITY TO CARRIER								
	A. C No							
PRE CARRIAGE BY	PLACE OF RECEIPT	EXPORTERS REF 243607		AGENTS REF				
OCEAN VESSEL SEVEN SEAS	PORT OF LOADING FELIXSTOWE	ORIGIN OF SHIPMENT		FOR CM USE ONLY				
PORT OF DISCHARGE NEW YORK	PLACE OF DELIVERY	FREIGHT PAYABLE AT MANCHESTER						
MARKS & NUMBERS N.Y BOOKS 31642 MANHATTAN NEW YORK	CONTAINER No	No. of PKGS DESCRIPTION OF GOODS 1 PAL BOX PRINTED EDUC. BOOKS		WEIGHT 500KG	MEASURE 1.030CM			

Bill of Exchange

No. .... Exchange for £ .... London ....

At .... after day pay this Second of Exchange.

First unpaid, to the Order of ....

....

payable at the current rate of exchange for sight drafts on London with Bank Commission, Colonial Stamp, Postages and all Charges Value received.

To .... For and on behalf of
OUP
.... Credit Controller

....

There will also be a *customs declaration form*. This contains a description of the goods being purchased and their country of origin.

Stock control

Knowing how much to purchase

How does Sally Johnston at The Village Stores (page 59) know what to order each week from the wholesaler? Although The Village Stores is a small shop, it still stocks a large range of goods and it would be very easy for Sally to run out of an item. Sally has neither the finance nor the space for a large stock so it is particularly important that she keeps a careful check on the goods she has in the shop. She does this by using stock record cards on which she records the amount of stock coming into the shop and the amount of stock which has been sold. She regularly updates the cards by checking the items on the shelves.

Sally is considering investing in a small microcomputer which has a program for stock control. Sally would need to input the data each week and the computer will remind her which goods she needs to order. Many firms now use computerised stock control methods. We will see in Unit 11 how important it is to maintain the correct levels of stock in a large manufacturing company in order to produce a steady flow off finished goods.

Bar coding: the latest in stock control

Some shops are now using light-sensitive pens or windows to read the bar codes on products. The information is rapidly fed into a computer at the cash desk and this prints out the price of the good. This has several advantages:

a it saves time at the checkout,

b each item does not need to be individually priced,

c the computer records what has been sold and this information is then used to indicate the levels of stock in the shop at any given moment.

Point of sale (POS) stock-keeping is likely to become more frequently used in the future in large shops. It is, however, expensive — costing up to £10 000 per checkout.

Summary of key words and ideas

Methods of purchasing

- *Cash on delivery (COD)*   The purchaser must pay for the goods at the time of delivery.
- *Cash discount*   A reduction in the price of the goods given for prompt payment.
- *Credit*   When the purchaser pays for the goods over a period of time.
- *Interest*   A charge made on top of the cash price for buying on credit.
- *Interest-free credit*   When the purchaser is given credit and no extra charge is made above the cash price. It is to the advantage of the purchasers if they are offered interest-free credit because they retain the use of their money for an extra period of time.
- *Hire purchase*   The purchaser makes a deposit and pays for the goods over a period of time in instalments. The goods do not belong to the purchaser until s/he has completed paying for them.
- *Finance Company*   An organisation that arranges HP.
- *Leasing*   A form of long-term renting of assets, such as vehicles and machines. The leasing firm is responsible for the repair and maintainance.
- It often pays small firms to hire equipment rather than purchase it if the equipment is very expensive or not often used.

Documents used in purchasing

- *The order*   Form on which the purchaser lists requirements.
- *Delivery note*   Document containing details of the goods being delivered.
- *The invoice*   Document giving all the details of the order including price, quantity, VAT, etc.
- *Credit note*   Sent by the seller if the purchaser has been overcharged.
- *Debit note*   Sent by the seller if the purchaser has been undercharged.
- *Monthly statement*   Shows on their account how much the purchaser owes.
- *Receipt*   Sent by the seller when the purchaser has paid for the goods.
- *Bill of exchange*   Used to finance overseas purchases.
- *Bill of lading*   Document giving ownership of goods in shipment.
- *Air waybill*   Used for air freight to show ownership of goods.
- *Stock control*   A check on the level of stock needed in the business.
- *Stock record cards*   Method of recording information on how much stock is in the business at any one time.

Suggestions for coursework

1 Choose two items which are normally available on HP or rental terms (eg televisions, video recorders, etc.) Compare the cost of buying by cash with HP or renting for a year. List the possible advantages and disadvantages of each method.

2 For either a real or an imaginary business, draw up the appropriate documents used in purchasing, showing how a particular order is processed.

Test questions on obtaining equipment and supplies

1 John Draper, self-employed electrician, has been offered some equipment on '3 months interest-free credit'.
   a What does '3 months interest free credit' mean?
   b What would John need to check before taking on the credit?
   c What are the advantages of interest-free credit for John?
2 You are the owner of a small bakery which makes deliveries to shops and cafes in the locality. You need to use two vans. List the advantages and disadvantages of
   a buying the vans by cash,
   b buying them on HP,
   c leasing them.
3 Suggest an appropriate method of purchasing the following items giving reasons for your choice:
   a cars for sales representatives,
   b stocks of raw materials,
   c extension to existing buildings,
   d payment of wages without enough cash in your bank account to cover them.
4 Marcia Lloyd manages a knitwear shop. She orders her supplies from a wholesaler called Scottish Woolmasters. List and describe any four documents that would pass between Marcia and Scottish Woolmasters after she places an order.
5 How would a supplier correct an error on an invoice if s/he had overcharged a customer on an invoice?
6 Explain how Quickbuild, a small firm of builders, might make use of each of the methods of purchasing illustrated for obtaining items for their business.

Extension questions

1 Describe any two documents that would be used if goods are bought from overseas.

2 Study the invoice shown and answer the following questions:

```
JMB Supplies Ltd                    Invoice No 1826
Wingate
Norwich                             10 March 1988
Norfolk
                                    Your Order No 967

Arcadia Nurseries                   Terms: Cash 5%
The Avenue                                 One Month 2½%
Bromley
Kent                                Carr. Paid
```

Qty	Description	Unit Prices	Total
5 Doz	Grow Bags	2.30	138.00
3 Doz	Peat Pots	0.50	18.00

    a Who is the supplier?
    b Who is the purchaser?
    c What has been supplied?
    d At what stage would an invoice be sent?
    e What is the purpose of the invoice?
    f What does 'Carr. paid' mean?
    g What does 'Terms: cash 5%, One month $2\frac{1}{2}\%$' mean?
    h What is a trade discount given for?

3 a What is the purpose of stock control?
    b Explain how computers could be used to aid stock control in a large supermarket.

4 **a** Explain how the shop shown in the illustration below might apply
stock control.

  b 'Too much stock is as bad as too little'. Explain why this might be
the case in the context of this shop.

  c How might the method of stock control be different in a large,
modern supermarket?

Unit 7 Selling the product

aims At the end of this unit you should understand:

▶ The methods of sales promotion.
▶ The purposes and methods of advertising.
▶ The idea of product differentiation.
▶ How firms decide upon a price.
▶ The idea of a marketing mix.
▶ The different channels of distribution.

(*Note* Market research for the small business is referred to in Unit 2 (page 18) and is returned to in Section III Unit 14 along with other aspects of selling in a large firm)

The Wooden Toy Company Ltd

exercise You are the marketing manager for The Wooden Toy Company Ltd. The firm makes handcrafted specialist wooden toys. Currently its three main products are:

1 a railway engine which can be assembled by a three-year old,
2 a clown which balances and rotates between parallel rails,
3 a miniature rocking horse and rider.

A new managing director has just taken over at The Wooden Toy Company and you receive the following memo:

```
        MEMO                    Date: 29-9-88

from: Managing Director
to:   Marketing Manager

Ref: Sales figs. 1986-8 (attached)

You will notice from the enclosed figures that
total sales have been virtually static for the
past three years despite a growing toy market.
I am very keen to improve upon our sales in the
next financial year and to show improved profits
to our shareholders.  Please prepare a new
marketing plan setting out three alternative
strategies for Wooden Toys, giving your views on
the suitability of each strategy.
```

SALES FIGURES 1986 - 8			
	1986	1987	1988
Railway Engine	4025	5982	6745
Clown	5673	4031	4021
Rocking Horse	6514	5821	4954
Other toys	2384	2518	2427
Total sales	18596	18352	18147

exercise   Your task as marketing manager is to carry out the instruction in the memo from the managing director. In the time given (one year) it will be very difficult for the firm to switch into a completely new product outside the wooden toy range. It may well be possible, however, to develop a new type of wooden toy. The first thing you do is to jot down *all* the possible ways of improving your firm's sales in the next year.

Increase advertising   New wooden toy   Reduce price
Improve existing   (market research)   Increase sales
designs   outlets
    Toy fairs   Increase
        salesmen
Improve packaging   Sell by mail order
????????   ????????   ????????

From your jottings you construct different plans. Against each plan you list the possible disadvantages. At the end of your report you recommend one particular strategy.

Increasing sales

The exercise on The Wooden Toy Company should have given you some idea of the range of things which can influence a firm's sales. Using the example of The Wooden Toy Company we will now look at some of these influences in turn.

Advertising

Purpose

Advertising is a very large industry in the UK. Each year firms in the UK spend approximately £3½ billion on advertising. Much of this is spent by the large firms (see Unit 14) but even quite small firms often spend a considerable proportion of their budget on advertising.

Advertising by firms is a way of increasing sales of their products or services. Advertising is also used to launch a new product and to keep the name of a product in the public's mind. It attempts to do this in two ways:

a by *informing* them about the product and making the consumer aware that the product exists,

b by trying to *persuade* the consumer that they need a particular product or service and that their product or service is the best on the market.

exercise

1 Look at the following example of an advertisement for The Wooden Toy Company that appeared in a local newspaper.

Give something different this Christmas

Superb hand-crafted traditional wooden toys. Made in our own workshops from only the highest quality hardwoods.

Every child will be delighted to receive a present from our range of interesting and educational wooden toys.

Available in good toy shops or direct from The Wooden Toy Company

a List all the facts given which inform the consumer about the firm's products.

b List the statements that attempt to persuade the consumer that they need Wooden Toy products.

c Carry out the same exercise for advertisements of your choice from a newspaper or magazine.

d Design an advertisement for a new soft drink which contains both factual information about the product and also attempts to persuade the consumer to buy it.

Types of advertising for the small business

exercise

Task 1 Using the pictures below to assist you, list all the places advertisements appear.

Here are some examples of the costs of different types of advertising in 1987.

Postcard in a newsagent's window	30p per week
Small ad in 'free' newspaper	8p per word
Local newspaper (circulation 33 000)	£500 full page
Local newspaper (circulation 110 000)	£1 400 full page
The Times (circulation 470 000)	£11 500 full page
The Sun (circulation 4 000 000)	£26 000 full page
60-second advert on local radio off-peak £550	
60-second advert on local radio peak rate £850	
60-second TV advert off-peak £10 000	
60-second TV advert peak viewing £61 000	

Task 2 Of the methods of advertising you have listed in *Task 1*, which do you consider to be appropriate for the small business?

Apart from the cost, firms must consider the likely market for their product or service. It would be unwise, for example, for a village store to go to the expense of advertising in a national newspaper when most of the readers are not going to be living near the shop. Firms which do not sell direct to the public often advertise in *trade journals* which are read by people specialising in a particular product or service, eg the grocery trade, electrical services, etc.

Task 3 Suggest appropriate forms of advertising for,
a a small hair salon,
b a window cleaner,
c a chain of 12 bakeries located in one region of the country,
d a food wholesaler selling only to shops,
e a small manufacturer of clothing kits sold direct to the public by mail order.

Pricing

How do firms go about deciding upon the price of their product? Choosing the correct price will be crucial to selling the product. One way of fixing the price is to take the average cost of making the product (see Unit 4) and to add on a profit. This method is known as *mark-up pricing*. This is the approach adopted by Wooden Toys. The average cost of making and selling their railway engine is £4.00. They add on 25%, which would give a selling price of £5. They actually sell it at £4.99. (Why do you suppose they reduce the price by 1 penny?).

How do firms decide upon how much to mark up their products by? Why does Wooden Toys add on 25% and not 50% or 10%? An important factor here will be how much any rival firms are charging for similar products. If Wooden Toys charge a great deal more for their railway engine than similar products on the market they are clearly not going to sell many. At the same time they must ask themselves whether they will sell many more if they greatly reduce the price. If they make the price too low, people may think that there is something wrong with the product.

exercise Wooden Toys currently sells its railway engine at £4.99. At this price it has been selling an average of 130 engines a week. A rival firm has cut the price of its similar engine to £4.75 and this has reduced sales of Wooden Toy's engine to an average of 100 a week. As marketing manager of Wooden Toys, you are considering reducing the price of your engine. You have estimated the following sales figures:

Price	Expected sales (weekly average)
£4.99	100
£4.80	103
£4.75	120
£4.70	130
£4.60	132

a Why is a large increase in sales expected if the price is reduced from £4.80 to £4.75?

b What price would you recommend for Wooden Toy's engine, assuming that production costs remain the same?

c At the new price would Wooden Toys be better or worse off than they were before their rivals cut their price?

d What might the rival's reaction be to Wooden Toys new price?

e What other options might be open to Wooden Toys, apart from changing price?

f What might happen to Wooden Toys' prices and sales if the rival firm went out of business?

Other methods of sales promotion

Apart from advertising and reducing their price, what other methods could Wooden Toys adopt to gain a larger share of the market? One possibility is for them to stress the differences between their products and their rivals. This is known as *product differentiation*. The differences may be real or the consumer may be persuaded by advertising that there are differences.

> ## Wooden Toys
>
> *The Different Toys!*
>
> Hand crafted – no machines used
>
> *
>
> Made individually by one
> craftsman – no production line
>
> *
>
> Made to the highest specification
> – no corner cutting

exercise How are Wooden Toys trying to differentiate their products from other toys?

Products can also be made to look different or more attractive by clever *packaging*. Wooden Toys might adopt more eye-catching colours and better looking boxes for the packaging of their products.

The ways in which Wooden Toys sells its products to the consumer are important. The more *retail outlets* it has, the better its chances of selling its products. Wooden Toys currently employs two sales representatives who visit toy shops in order to try and persuade them to stock its products. Each year a number of *toy fairs* are held where toy manufacturers display their products to buyers from shops. Wooden Toys could certainly consider the possibility of attending more of these in order to try and increase the number of shops where their products are sold.

The last section of this unit looks at different methods of selling to the public by looking at the various channels of distribution.

The marketing mix

We have seen that there are a large number of ingredients which go into selling a product or service: advertising, pricing, the range of products, packaging, retail outlets, salesmen, market research and aftersales service. The way in which these ingredients are combined for a particular product is called the *marketing mix*. The mix will vary considerably between products — the mix will be very different for a machine to be sold to a manufacturer from that of a soft toy to be sold through shops to the consumer.

Fullerton's Fudge

Fullertons, a small sweet manufacturer, have been making fudge for the past 50 years. It is packaged in rather boring and unattractive plastic bags. It is only sold in shops within a radius of 30 miles from the factory. It is not surprising that Fullerton's Fudge has a rather small and, recently, declining market.

exercise
a As the recently appointed marketing manager you have been asked to come up with a new image for Fullerton's Fudge. The basic product will remain the same but you will need to design new packaging and a new poster advertisement for it.
b Suggest other ways of improving the marketing of Fullerton's Fudge, paying particular attention to the marketing mix.
c Write a memo to your sales representatives indicating the new image you wish them to try and create for Fullerton's Fudge when they visit retailers who have not previously stocked the product.

The channels of distribution

Where are we going to sell our products?
Having made our goods, how are we going to get them to the consumer?

Direct selling

Many small manufacturing firms sell direct to the consumer. Ling's Pottery in Unit 5 is a good example of direct selling to the public. She was both the manufacturer and the *retailer* (the place where goods are sold to the public).

For some manufacturers the consumer may be another manufacturing firm. A small firm may make components for a larger firm. In this case the small firm will often sell direct to the large manufacturer.

Door-to-door salespeople

Some small firms may employ *door-to-door salespeople* who carry a stock of goods or advertising information about the goods and call on selected houses in an area. A very small firm, such as a one-person business, might employ this method of selling. It is also used by large organisations such as Avon Cosmetics and Everest Double Glazing.

Telephone selling

A recent development in the UK, has been *telephone selling*. The firm employs staff who telephone members of the public and try and persuade them to purchase goods. This has tended to be used by larger firms, but some small firms use a telephone-selling agency as a way of selling their goods.

Mail order

Mail order is another method of direct selling used by both small and large firms. Large firms may produce expensive catalogues which can be used by the consumer to order the goods of their choice. Small firms may simply place an advertisement in the local paper inviting customers to buy direct from the firm through the post. This was one method of selling used by The Wooden Toy Company earlier in this unit.

Selling through a middleman

It is often very expensive for manufacturing firms to sell in small quantities to a large range of consumers. These firms will often sell through a middleman. The middleman buys in bulk from the manufacturer and breaks this into smaller quantities to be sold to the final customers. A *wholesaler* is a type of middleman. You may remember that Ramesh Patel in Unit 6 bought the goods he required for his corner shop from a cash-and-carry wholesaler. This is where retailers visit the wholesaler and transport their own goods. Other wholesalers, like that used by Sally Johnston in Unit 6, operate a delivery service for retailers.

Some manufacturers may use *selling agencies* to distribute their goods for them. The selling agency acts for a number of manufacturers who find it cheaper to operate through a specialist in selling. This is particularly the case when small firms wish to sell overseas (see Unit 6).

questions

1 What advantages are there for
   a the manufacturer,
   b the retailer,
   using a wholesaler?
2 Why does the use of a wholesaler normally result in higher prices for the customer?
3 What is meant by a 'cash-and-carry' wholesaler?

Types of retail outlets

exercise Match the following definitions of types of retail outlets to the pictures and titles:

Definitions

1 A collection of rented stalls selling a range of goods. Often held outdoors in the centre of a town either daily or once a week.

2 A coin-operated machine supplying items like drinks, sandwiches and sweets. Often found on stations and in other public places.

3 A vehicle that sells goods in a variety of places. Most common in rural areas where there is a lack of shops. Often sells food such as fish, fruit and bread.

4 A small shop, often a sole-owner business. Very often a corner shop, general stores or newsagent.

5 One of ten or more shops under the same ownership. Examples include Marks and Spencer, Woolworths, Boots, Dixons.

6 Normally large shops in the centre of towns selling a very wide variety of goods. There are normally a large number of shop assistants in each section. There are often several floors in these shops.

7 These are large shops on one level with a floor area of more than 2000 square feet. They sell food but are increasingly stocking other household items. Self-service for most items is usual and they are often located outside town centres with large car parking facilities. Leading examples include Sainsbury and Presto.

8 Very large shops with more than 50 000 square feet of floor space. They are located on the outskirts of towns with very extensive car parking facilities. Apart from food, they often sell electrical goods, garden supplies and clothes. Asda and Carrefour are both developing this type of store.

9 Located on the outskirts of towns, often in industrial estates. Customers select items, such as furniture, which are collected from a large store. Examples include MFI and Queensway. Prices are often lower than those in town-centre shops.

Retail outlets

a mobile shop

b independent

e chain store

c discount warehouse

d supermarket

h vending machine

f market

g hypermarket

i department store

The continuing story of Fullertons

At present Fullertons sell their sweets direct to local shops without using a wholesaler. As marketing manager you wish to increase the number of retail outlets stocking Fullerton's products. Selling outside of the present locality will either involve employing more salesmen to visit new shops or using wholesalers to distribute the sweets for them. Using more salesmen will be costly as they need to be equipped with vehicles. Using wholesalers will require fewer salesmen and has the added advantage of supplying easy access to a large number of retailers who already visit the wholesalers. The main drawback of using the wholesalers is that, because the wholesalers need to make a profit, the price to the consumer will be higher unless Fullertons are prepared to make less profit on each packet of sweets they sell.

questions

1 What advantages will there be for Fullertons using wholesalers rather than selling direct to retailers?
2 What costs will be reduced by using wholesalers?
3 Explain why using a wholesaler will mean either higher prices for the consumer or less profit per packet of sweets for Fullertons.
4 Can you think of any other disadvantages for Fullertons of using wholesalers rather than direct selling by salesmen?
5 Fullertons might also consider using mail order as a method of selling. What is mail order? What advantages are there for Fullertons of this method of selling? Which costs would be saved by this method of selling compared to using salesmen or wholesalers? What extra costs would there be if mail order selling was used?

The small firm and retail outlets

Most small firms making products to be sold to the public will either sell direct, use wholesalers or sell to small shops. The large chain stores and supermarkets need to buy in bulk and the small manufacturer is often unable to produce in sufficient quantity or at low enough prices to compete with the larger manufacturers. Some small specialist manufacturers do manage to win contracts to supply the large retailers. This has been the case with Betta Pies, a small bakery, which has supplied fresh meat pies and quiches to leading supermarkets.

There are three ways however in which small retail businesses can appeal to a wider range of customers.

Franchising

This is when a business buys a licence or franchise to operate as a well-known firm. This is often the case in the fast food trade where businesses buy franchises to operate as Wimpy Bars, Kentucky Fried Chicken, etc.

Voluntary trading groups

The best-known example is SPAR shops. The shops are owned privately, often as sole-owner businesses, and they join the SPAR organisation. SPAR buys products from the manufacturers, often obtaining a bulk discount similar to the large supermarkets, and sells to the member shops often under their own label. This means that the small retailer benefits from using a well-known name and from lower prices from the manufacturer.

In-store boutiques

Some large department stores rent floor space to other businesses wishing to display their products. This is sometimes the case for cosmetics, household products and food. The in-store boutique benefits from being in a large shop which attracts many customers. Although they need to pay rent to the department store, the boutique does not have to pay all the overhead costs of a large shop in a town centre.

Cosmetics companies often rent specialist counters in large department stores

Summary of key words and ideas

- *Marketing* Finding and developing the right product, getting the product from the manufacturer to the consumer using advertising, packaging, pricing, salesmen and other methods of sales promotion.
- *Advertising* attempts both to *inform* customers of a product or service and to *persuade* them to purchase it.
- There are many different types of advertising appearing in a wide range of places. The cost of advertising varies directly with the expected size of audience. Firms will take account of costs and the type of audience they are trying to reach when selecting methods of advertising.
- *Mark-up pricing* is calculated by taking average costs and adding a profit % to it. The % mark-up will depend upon such factors as the prices competitors are charging and the amount people are prepared to pay for the good or service. *Product differentiation* is an attempt by a firm to distinguish its product or service from that of its rivals.
- *Retail outlet* The place where goods are sold to the public as consumers.
- *The marketing mix* The way in which the various aspects of sales promotion are combined in marketing a product. The mix will vary depending upon the nature of the product and the market it is intended for.
- *Sales Representatives* People employed by the firm to sell its products or services to customers.
- *Direct Selling* When the firm sells its products to the final consumer without going through any middlemen. Methods include door-to-door salesmen, mail order and telephone selling. This may reduce costs for the firm but it may not reach such a wide market.
- *Wholesalers* Middlemen between the manufacturer and the customers. They buy in bulk from the firm and break this into smaller units for the customer. The wholesaler may save the firm transport costs and help it to reach a wider market.
- *Channels of distribution* The ways in which goods reach the final consumer from the manufacturer.
- Small firms can become better known by using franchising, voluntary trading organisations and by renting accommodation from large stores.

Suggestions for coursework

1 Show how you would go about marketing a product of your choice including the product design, the advertising, packaging, channels of distribution and any other relevant aspects of sales promotion.
2 Carry out a survey of advertising to show,
   a the range of advertising,
   b how different types of firms use different forms of advertising,
   c the methods employed by advertisers,
   d how television advertising varies with the time of day and the likely audience.

3 Conduct a survey to test reactions to advertising:
   a List five catch phrases or names of well-known personalities from advertisements and find out how many people connect them with the right product.
   b Find out which brands of various common household products people use and why they use them in order to check the influence of advertising.
   c Find out how people regard advertising. Does advertising entertain, spoil good programmes, put up prices, inform, persuade you to buy things you do not require, mislead, etc?

4 Make a comparison of shops in a town centre with those in a village or suburb of a town. Compare types of shops and what they sell.
   Carry out a survey to see,
   a how frequently people shop,
   b where they shop for particular goods,
   c why they use particular shops.

Test questions on selling

1 The Standard Pen Company Ltd. is a small manufacturer of writing implements (fountain pens, propelling pencils, etc.) Its products tend to be rather traditional in design. Recently sales have been falling as a result of increased competition.
   Suggest four different ways in which the Standard Pen Company could regain its share of the market, explaining how each method might attract extra customers.

2 'Advertising attempts both to inform and to persuade'.
   a Explain how advertising attempts to sell more goods and services.
   b Explain how the following advertisement attempts both to inform and to persuade the consumer.

> ### The Standard Ink Master Pen
>
> A traditional pen made to the highest quality by our skilled craftsmen. Each pen is individually produced in our own workshops using only the finest materials.
>
> Make sure that your writing is at its best by buying the best.
> Available at quality retailers £6.50

   c How is the Standard Pen Company trying to differentiate its product?

3 Alek has recently started a small hairdressing business in the suburbs of a large town. He has allowed himself £500 a year for advertising and promotion. Advise him on how best to use the money. Include three different methods of advertising and sales promotion in your advice.

4 You are the owner of a greengrocers.
   a Describe two things you might take into account when deciding on the price of oranges in your shop.

b The price of a large orange is currently 15p. You calculate that if you were to reduce the price to 10p you would sell 20% more oranges. Should you reduce the price? Explain your answer.

5 **a** Describe two ways in which a firm could sell direct to the customer without using any middlemen.

  b Give two advantages and two disadvantages of this selling method.

6 Some firms sell by mail order.

  a What does this mean?

  b What costs does the firm save by using mail order?

  c What extra costs does this method of selling involve for the firm?

7 'A wholesaler is a middleman'.

  a Explain what this means.

  b Describe two advantages of a firm selling through a wholesaler rather than selling direct.

8 'The Corner Shop' is a small independent general store located in the suburbs of a large city. The owner purchases stock at a local cash-and-carry wholesalers. In general its prices are higher by about 10% than the nearest supermarket which is two miles away.

  a What is meant by an *independent* shop?

  b What is a cash-and-carry wholesaler?

  c Give two reasons why prices in The Corner Shop are 10% higher than those in the supermarket.

  d Give two reasons why people still shop at The Corner Shop rather than go to the cheaper supermarket.

9 **a** Give an example of a multiple chain store.

  b Why is it often difficult for a small manufacturer to get its goods sold in a large multiple?

  c What advantages are there for a firm selling its goods through a multiple?

Extension questions

1 D H Philips is a large department store in the centre of a major town. MID is a cash-and-carry discount warehouse on the outskirts of the same town. Both retail outlets sell furniture but MID is considerably cheaper.

  a What is a department store?

  b What is a cash-and-carry discount warehouse?

  c Why is MID cheaper for furniture?

  d Why will people still buy at D H Philips?

2 Recently a company has applied for planning permission to build a new hypermarket on the outskirts of a market town.

  a What is a hypermarket?

  b Why are hypermarkets normally located on the outskirts of towns?

  c What arguments are there for and against the building of the hypermarket?

3 Describe how the marketing mix of a new board game might be different from that of an industrial carpet-cleaning service.

Section III

The large firm

Unit 8   Expanding the business

aims   At the end of this unit you should understand:

▶   The importance of large firms in the UK economy.
▶   Why firms wish to expand.
▶   The advantages and disadvantages of firms becoming larger.
▶   How firms expand.
▶   How public limited companies are formed and operate.
▶   How large companies are financed.
▶   The purpose and function of the Stock Exchange.

The importance of the large firm

In Section II we have been looking at small firms employing less than 50 people. Small firms are very important in the UK economy, particularly for employment. 60% of people working in the private sector of the UK economy work for firms employing less than 50 people. At the same time, large firms produce 60% of the UK's manufacturing output. The importance of large companies is also growing. The top 100 companies in the UK produce 70% of total manufacturing output compared to 60% 10 years ago. In some industries, a very small number of firms produce most of the output.

The case of the UK washing powder industry

All of the above examples of washing powders are produced by just two companies: Proctor and Gamble and Unilever, who together make over 90% of all washing powders, as well as many other soap products.

questions   1 What disadvantages could there be for the consumer of only having two major producers of washing powders?
2 What advantages are there for Proctor and Gamble and Unilever of being the only two major producers of washing powders?

extension exercise   1 How do the two washing powder firms compete with each other when they advertise? Do they compete in price or mainly in other ways?
2 Why do you think competition takes this form?

Why do firms wish to expand?

Many firms are content to remain as small businesses, while for others expansion seems to be the main aim of the firm. There are many good examples today of large firms which started in a very small way in the past.

Richard Branson, multi-million pound founder of Virgin Records and Virgin Atlantic Airways, started by trading second-hand records and producing a school newspaper.

Alan Sugar, multi-million pound founder of Amstrad, started by selling aerials from the boot of his car.

Marks and Spencer started life as a market stall, and Boots the Chemist developed from one shop in Nottingham.

What motivated the owners of these businesses to grow larger?

- *Greater profits* Normally, as a firm grows larger, it increases its turnover and adds to its profits. Most large companies are owned by shareholders and they benefit from the company making increased profits. Increased profits often encourage more people to buy shares in the company and this gives the firm more money for expansion.
- *The desire to dominate the market* The larger the share of total output a firm has of a particular product, the more it can control prices. When there is only one major producer of a particular product, the firm is called a *monopoly*. (We will see in Unit 16 that the Government attempts to control monopolies because they are obviously in a very powerful position and could exploit the consumer).
- *The personal satisfaction gained* Apart from increasing their profits, owners may gain satisfaction from seeing their company grow larger.
- *Diversification* When some firms expand they *diversify*. This means that they start producing a range of products or services different from the one they started with.

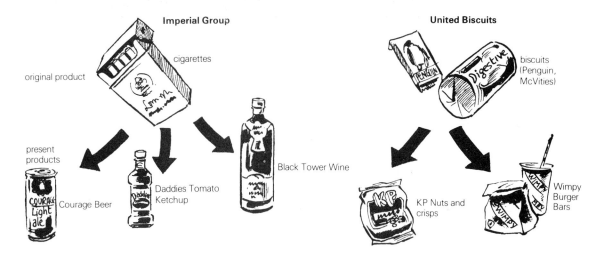

- *The economies of large-scale production* Some firms expand in order to gain what are known as the *economies of scale*. These are the advantages to the firm of increasing its size. A firm gaining economies of scale will see its average costs fall as it increases production. For example, 100 units may cost £400 (average cost = £4) while 1000 units may cost £3000 (average cost = £3).

What are the economies of scale?

case study

The example of Taylor's fuel service

Ten years ago, Taylors was a small firm delivering fuel oil to homes in its local area. Taylors is now a company with a nationwide network of fuel delivery services which includes coal and butane gas in addition to fuel oil. The expansion of Taylors illustrates many of the economies of scale. They now buy their fuels in larger amounts from the suppliers. Buying in bulk normally means lower prices. In addition to this, Taylors now have greater bargaining power when dealing with their suppliers.

Taylors now use much larger oil tankers for delivery. An oil tanker which is capable of carrying 20 000 gallons does not cost twice as much as one which will only carry 10 000 gallons. An oil tanker of 20 000 gallons will cost more per mile to run than one of 10 000 gallons, but will not cost twice as much.

Taylors now advertise in the national press and on television. This is much more expensive than when they only advertised locally, but they now reach a much wider audience. Taylors can now afford to employ specialists to help run the business more efficiently. They now have their own experts in purchasing, marketing and finance.

questions

1 List all the benefits Taylors have gained as a result of expanding.
2 What do you think is meant by 'greater bargaining power'?
3 Why will an oil tanker of 20 000 gallons not cost twice as much to purchase or to run as one of 10 000 gallons?
4 How has Taylors diversified its service? What benefits might this bring to Taylors?

Other examples of economies of scale

- Large firms find it easier to raise finance.
- Large firms can afford to employ scientists and researchers to develop new and better products.
- Large firms can employ expensive equipment because the size of their output means that they can use it to its maximum capacity.
- Large firms can divide work up more easily into specialist departments.

Diseconomies of scale: the disadvantages of producing on a large scale

Although there are many advantages of large-scale production, there may also be some disadvantages caused by a firm expanding.

- Firms may become very complicated in their organisation and find it difficult to make decisions quickly.
- The management may lose contact with workers in the factory and this may lead to poor working relationships, which may in turn lead to less efficient work.
- Large firms are often less flexible than small firms. Small firms may find it easier to switch production to meet a new fashion than large firms.
- Communications between people in large firms often become more difficult and involve more paperwork and meetings. All this requires more in the way of administrators and secretarial staff.

How do firms expand?

There are basically two ways in which a firm can grow larger:
- By expanding on its own, taking an increasing share of a market, or entering new ones, by diversification of products or services. Firms do this by being more competitive than their rivals or by offering a better product or service. This has been true of firms such as Sainsbury — which now accounts for 12% of all grocery trade in the UK.

SAINSBURY'S
Half-Year Results

£ million	1986 28 weeks to 4th October	1985 28 weeks to 5th October	Increase
Sales*	2,087.6	1,831.6	14.0%
Retail Profit	115.1	85.2	35.1%
Retail Margin	5.51%	4.65%	
Associates	8.5	7.2	17.1%
Group Profit before Tax	123.5	92.4	33.7%
Group Profit after Estimated Tax	80.3	60.1	33.7%
Earnings per Share (at 35% tax)	11.38p	8.60p	32.3%
Dividend per Share	2.05p	1.65p	24.2%

*Includes VAT

Profits up by one third

- By buying up other companies through *take-overs* and *mergers*. A take-over is when one company buys enough shares in another firm to gain control of it. A merger is when companies agree to join together under one board of management. Where a firm has acquired a number of other companies which retain their original names, it is known as a *holding company*. Imperial Group are an example of a holding company.

Extension section

Types of Integration (joining together of firms)

There are two types of integration

- *Horizontal* Firms at the *same* stage of production join together, eg two manufacturing firms join together or two service industries amalgamate.
- *Vertical* Firms at *different* stages of production join together, eg a manufacturer buys up a supplier of raw materials, or a manufacturer buys up a chain of shops. Vertical integration can be further divided into *forwards vertical* (where a firm joins together with one in a *later* stage of production) and *backwards vertical* (where a firm joins together with one in a *previous* stage of production).

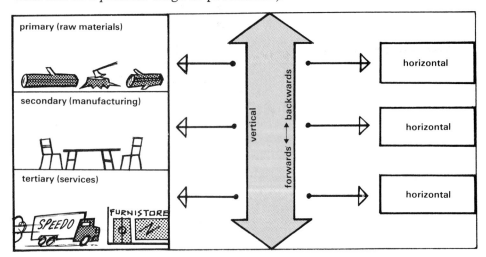

exercise *Which type of integration?*

Say whether each of the following mergers/take-overs is an example of horizontal or vertical integration. If you decide it is vertical, say whether it is backwards or forwards.

1 The merger of National Provincial Bank and Westminster Bank to form Nat West Bank.
2 Brook Bond Tea buying up tea plantations in Sri Lanka.
3 Scottish and Newcastle Brewery buying up public houses.
4 MFI, cash-and-carry discount furniture retailers, buying up Hygena, manufacturers of kitchen units.
5 Amstrad Electronics take-over of Sinclair Computers.

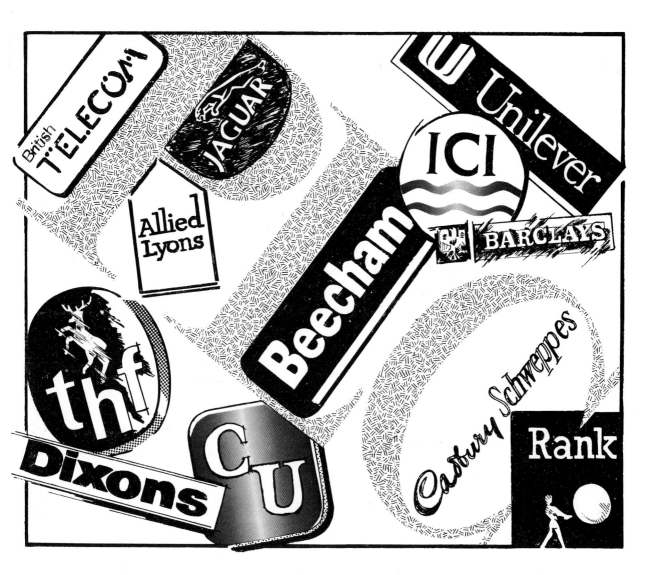

The public limited company

All of the above are examples of *Public Limited Companies*. Public Limited Companies have the letters PLC after their name. Any member of the public is entitled to buy shares in a Public Limited Company. The shares of UK public limited companies are bought and sold on the Stock Exchange (see the last section of this unit for details) and their prices are published in most national newspapers. (Some newspapers just show the main shares).

exercise

1 List the above companies and try to name at least one product or service produced by each.
2 Find the share prices in a newspaper and name two public limited companies in each of the primary, secondary and tertiary sectors of the economy.

91

Why form a public limited company?

Shares in *private limited companies* cannot be sold publicly. This limits the number of shares which can be easily sold and restricts the amount of finance available to the company. Public limited companies can advertise their shares and sell to the public and financial institutions (such as insurance companies) both in the UK and abroad. Public limited companies may have several million shares owned by a large number of different shareholders, ranging from individuals, with as few as 50 shares, to large financial institutions, which may own 100 000 shares or more.

Ownership of a public company

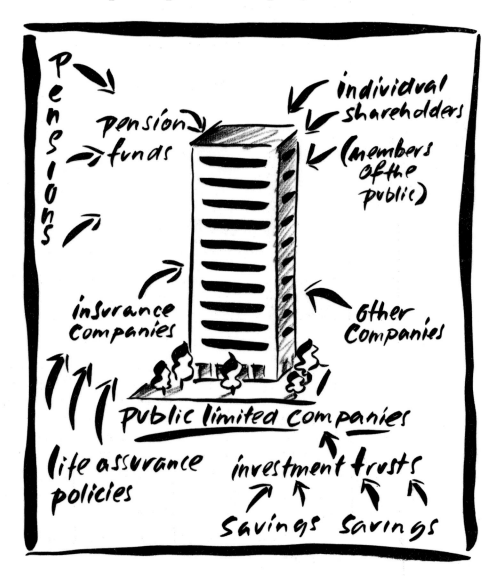

How are public limited companies formed?

Most public limited companies start as private limited companies. Because the shares in public limited companies are sold to the public, there are many more rules and regulations governing their formation and the way in which they operate. It is very expensive to form a public limited company and this type of business organisation is only open to private limited companies with a considerable amount of capital. Public limited companies need a minimum of £50 000 capital and often need to spend at least £250 000 on advertising, legal fees and commission.

Like private limited companies, the PLC must send its Articles and Memorandum of Association to the Registrar of Companies and apply for a trading certificate. It cannot start trading, however, until it has satisfied the Registrar that it has raised sufficient capital and has been approved by the Stock Exchange Council.

How are shares sold in a PLC?

VIRGIN GROUP plc

OFFER OF ORDINARY SHARES BY TENDER

ORGAN GRENFELL & CO. LIMITED

Virgin Group plc
(Registered in England No. 1568894)

Offer of Ordinary Shares by Tender

by

Morgan Grenfell & Co. Limited
as agent for the Company and the vendors whose names are set out herein

of up to 50,000,000 Ordinary Shares of 10p each to raise £60,000,000

with a minimum tender price of 120p per share

the amount tendered being payable in full on application

The company publishes a *prospectus* which sets out the background and details of the company, and what it hopes to achieve, so that the public can decide whether they wish to buy shares in the company.

Shares can be sold in the following ways:

- *Public issue* This is done by advertising in national newspapers, or elsewhere, inviting the public to buy shares in the company.
- *Private placing* This is when shares are sold to financial institutions, such as pension funds and insurance companies.
- *Rights issue* Shares are sold to existing shareholders. This is often the cheapest method because there is no need for an expensive prospectus or large-scale advertising.

As soon as a PLC starts trading, its shares can be bought and sold second-hand on the Stock Exchange.

(See last section of this Unit for how trading is carried out in the Stock Exchange.)

93

Running a public limited company

By law a Public Limited Company must:

- Have a minimum of two shareholders.
- Appoint a Board of Directors to manage the company.
- Hold an annual general meeting of shareholders.
- Give limited liability to its shareholders.
- Publish accounts each year in at least two national newspapers and send very detailed accounts of its affairs to the Registrar of Companies.
- Reveal what any subsidiary companies it owns are doing.
- State any donations to political parties and charities.
- Give details of changes in fixed assets (land and property bought and sold).

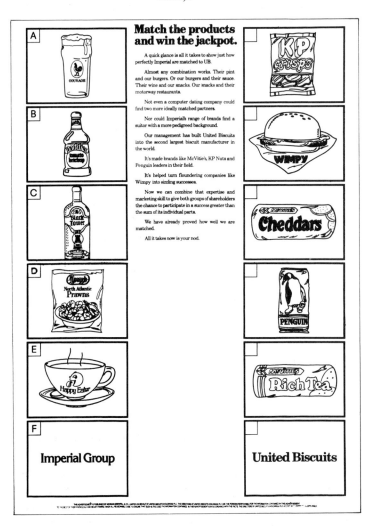

Management of the public limited company

The shareholders appoint a Board of Directors to manage the running of the company. The Board of Directors in turn appoint managers to carry out the day-to-day running of the company. The shareholders have the power to sack directors and must be consulted on major decisions, such as merging with other companies. In reality, in many cases, few shareholders bother to attend the annual general meeting. Often the shares are distributed between so many different people that control lies with one or two major institutions who own perhaps as little as 10% of the shares.

Proposed merger of Imperial Group and United Biscuits

This advertisement appeared in national newspapers in 1986.

questions

1. What are shareholders being asked to decide on?
2. Which way are the directors urging shareholders to vote?
3. What benefits do the directors claim will result from the proposal?
4. What disadvantages to the proposal might there be?

Financing large companies

Finance for large companies can either be *internal* (from within the company) or *external* (from outside the company).

Internal finance

- *Profits* Shareholders expect to receive a share in the profits of a company, but the company may retain some of its profits to reinvest in the company or use to purchase other firms. A sensible use of profits in this way may result in even greater dividends for shareholders in the future. Over half of all company finance comes from retained profits.
- *Sale of Assets* Companies may raise finance by selling off some of their assets. They may choose to sell whole firms which they have previously purchased or just parts (or 'divisions') of firms. Apart from raising finance, selling off unprofitable parts of a firm may increase the efficiency and profits of the firm. This is called *rationalisation*.

£52m for Unipart
By our Financial Editor

Rover, the vehicle group, yesterday announced the £52 million sale of its Unipart spare parts business to a consortium of City Institutions and employees.

It is thought that this is part of a rationalisation exercise by Rover to improve the firm's profitability as well as increase its capital position.

- *Sale of shares* A company going public will need to sell shares. An existing Public Limited Company may sell more shares to existing shareholders through a *rights issue* (see page 93).

Types of shares

There are several different types of shares available in public limited companies:

Ordinary shares (sometimes known as 'equities'). Ordinary shareholders are last to receive a *dividend* (see below) in the company's profits after other shareholders have been paid. All of the remaining profit is shared equally amongst ordinary shareholders depending upon the number of shares held. These are high-risk shares because there may not be any profit left in poor years after other shareholders have been paid. At the same time, ordinary shareholders can do very well if the company makes large profits.

- *Preference shares* These carry a fixed dividend which is paid out provided a profit is made by the company. They are less risky than ordinary shares because they are paid out before them, but preference shareholders do not have the opportunity of receiving large dividends on their shares as the rate of interest for them is fixed.
- *Cumulative preference shares* These are the same as preference shares, but if the company does not make profits in one year the dividend on the shares accumulates (builds up) and is paid out when the company does make enough profit.

Why buy shares?

- To receive a share of the profits. This is paid in the form of a *dividend* on each share owned.
- Shareholders hope that the price of their shares on the Stock Exchange will rise and that they will be able to sell them at a profit. This is known as making a capital gain. For example, it was possible to purchase shares in Amstrad for as little as 14p in 1984. The same shares in January 1987 were worth £1.36.
- To gain certain 'perks'. Some companies give shareholders benefits in order to encourage people to purchase shares and remain with the company. Examples include European Car Ferries, which gives shareholders discounts on ferry crossings to Europe, and British Telecom and British Gas giving vouchers to help pay for telephone and gas bills.
- To have a say in running the company. Each shareholder has one vote for each share owned. Large shareholders can influence company policy.

External finance

Like small firms, large companies can obtain finance from outside of the firm in the form of loans and grants.

Debentures

These are loans to the company by members of the public and financial institutions. They carry a fixed rate of interest. Some carry certain perks, eg debenture holders of the All England Club get priority for seats on the centre court at Wimbledon. Debenture holders are not owners of the company and do not have any voting rights or say in the management of the company. They must be paid interest before any shareholders because they are creditors of the company. The company may be declared bankrupt if the debenture holders cannot be paid. If the company is declared bankrupt, the debenture holders are compensated from the sale of assets before any shareholders.

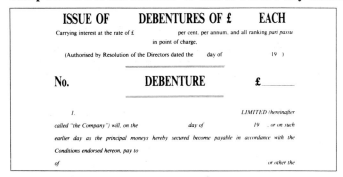

Other loans

Large firms obtain finance from a range of financial institutions:

- *Commercial banks*, such as Barclays, Lloyds, Nat West, etc, give overdrafts and loans (see Unit 5).
- *Merchant banks*   These are banks specialising in finance and do not deal with the ordinary public.
- *Insurance companies*   Insurance companies currently hold £6 billion worth of funds invested in life assurance policies. Insurance companies buy shares but also loan direct to industry.
- *Pension funds*   Huge amounts of money are held in pension funds, some of which is loaned to public limited companies.
- *The Government*   We have seen in Unit 5 how the Government makes loans to firms to encourage them to settle and expand in areas of high unemployment. The Government sometimes also makes loans to firms in financial difficulties in order to prevent them from going out of business and increasing unemployment. (This was the case with Rolls Royce and British Leyland.
- *The EEC*   The European Economic Community may give loans to firms, particularly in areas of high unemployment. Large grants have also been given for the improvement of firms, both large and small.

Extension section

Which type of finance?

Large companies generally use a range of different types of finance to suit different purposes.

case study

European Leisure PLC

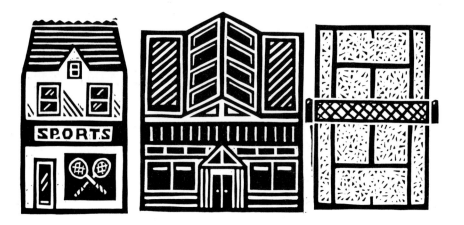

European Leisure is a rapidly expanding public limited company which owns sports shops, leisure centres and betting shops. It has been assisted in its expansion by Midland Bank which has given it a large overdraft facility as well as loans to help in its programme of building and developing leisure centres. European Leisure have a small number of debenture holders and their loans assist with the firm's need for working capital.

European Leisure is about to embark on a new phase of expansion by buying up a chain of travel agencies. European Leisure is a successful and profitable company and it intends to finance its acquisition through a rights issue of ordinary shares.

questions

1 What different types of finance does European Leisure use?
2 What is an 'overdraft facility'? What types of activity would it be used for?
3 What is meant by 'working capital'?
4 Why would European Leisure use debentures for working capital?
5 What is meant by a 'rights issue of ordinary shares'?
6 Why would people be keen to buy shares in European Leisure? What two benefits might they enjoy?
7 Why do you think European Leisure has chosen this method of raising finance to buy out the chain of travel agents?

The Stock Exchange

Bar Wars: now Rowntree shares soar by £50m

Rowntree shares soared by £50m on the stock market yesterday at the prospect of a three-way takeover battle for the company by Swiss confectionary giants Nestle and Suchard. Nestle are thought to be preparing to make an offer in the region of £2.1 billion for Rowntrees. Suchard, which currently holds 29.9 per cent of Rowntree shares, is also thought to be making a rival bid. Rowntree shares rose by 25p in trading yesterday. The Rowntree Board are strongly opposed to the takeover claiming that it will put jobs at risk and that will not be in the public interest. They want the bid referred to the Monopolies Commission for consideration . . .

The Stock Exchange is a market place where second-hand shares are bought and sold. The Stock Exchange is located in the City of London but it is linked by computer to other exchanges throughout the UK and abroad. Dealing and information on stocks and shares takes place through the Stock Exchange Automated Quotations System (SEAQ). Some six billion deals take place each year to the value of £350 billion on the Stock Exchange.

Shares can only be bought and sold by members of the Stock Exchange. Before 1986 there were two types of members; jobbers and brokers. In 1986 the Stock Exchange underwent a major change (known as the 'big bang'). One of the results of this has been the abolition of jobbers. Stockbrokers now deal direct with each other. Some stockbroking firms specialise in buying and selling shares and are known as *market makers*.

CHIEF PRICE CHANGES

RISES	p	p	FALLS	p	p
Feb International	154	+48	Sovereign Oil	59.50	−8.5
Entm. Prdn. Svcs.	25	+7	Humberside Eltn.	12	−1.5
Feb Intl. 'A'	104	+28	Maxiprint	22	−2
E.R.F. Holdings	76	+16	Lilleshall	193	−17
Isotron	235	+35	Norbain Eltn.	58	−5
Bramall, C.D.	183	+21	Lyles, S.	119	−10
Piccadilly Radio	40	+4	Upton, E.	50	−4
First Scty. Group	250	+25	ASDA-MFI Group	152	−12
Blackwood Hodge	50.25	+4.75	Cifer	24.75	−1.75
Clyde Blowers	215	+20	Grosvenor Square	150	−10

Guiness shares plummet

Amstrad shares rocket

T.S.B. oversubscribed six times

THE STOCK EXCHANGE

Stockbrokers can be contacted through banks or by obtaining a list of stockbroking firms from the Stock Exchange. Stockbrokers charge commission for either buying or selling shares. The amount charged can vary between brokers and differs according to the type and number of shares being bought and sold.

Stockbrokers must try to obtain the best possible deal for their clients. When they deal with other brokers they do not reveal whether they are buying or selling shares and will contact a number of broking firms in order to obtain the best price on the shares.

Stockbrokers also offer financial advice to clients, and help to manage various investment trusts and pension funds.

The *Stock Exchange Council* attempts to make sure that any company listed on the Stock Exchange comes up to certain standards and that dealings in shares are carried out correctly.

The *Unlisted Securities Market* is for some limited companies which fulfill certain conditions but which are not 'quoted' on the main Stock Exchange.

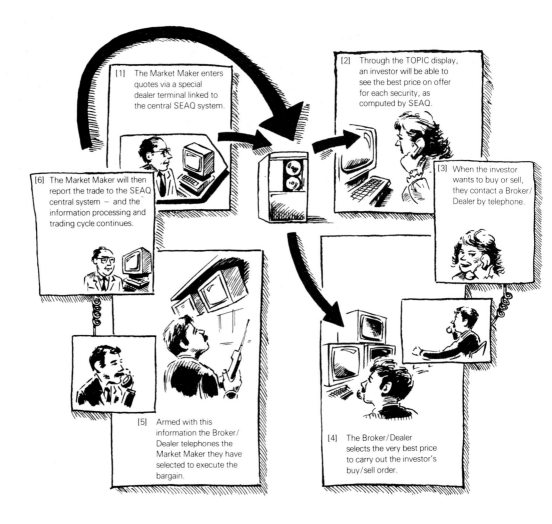

[1] The Market Maker enters quotes via a special dealer terminal linked to the central SEAQ system.

[2] Through the TOPIC display, an investor will be able to see the best price on offer for each security, as computed by SEAQ.

[3] When the investor wants to buy or sell, they contact a Broker/Dealer by telephone.

[4] The Broker/Dealer selects the very best price to carry out the investor's buy/sell order.

[5] Armed with this information the Broker/Dealer telephones the Market Maker they have selected to execute the bargain.

[6] The Market Maker will then report the trade to the SEAQ central system – and the information processing and trading cycle continues.

What makes share prices rise or fall?

Shares are like any other product in a *free market*. If they are in short supply (like fresh strawberries in the winter), their price will rise. This happened when shares in the Trustee Savings Bank were *over-subscribed* by six times when it went public.

There are various reasons why people start buying up a particular share:

- They expect the company to make large profits.
- The price of the share is low at the current time and it is expected to increase in the future.
- A company is expected to be taken over by another firm. (The firm carrying out the take-over will buy up the shares in the firm being taken over and this will push up the price of this firm's shares.)

exercise

How good an investor are you? Play the Stock Exchange Game.

You have inherited £1000 from a rich uncle who made a fortune on the Stock Exchange. He was keen that you should try your hand at gambling on shares and a condition of the will is that you invest the money in four companies listed on the Stock Exchange. Pick your four 'winners' from the shares listed in national newspapers. Check their progress over a period of one month. At the end of the month sell your shares and see if you have gained or lost. If you have gained, work the gain out as a percentage of your investment to see how this would have compared to investing £1000 in a bank or building society. (Remember to divide the bank or building society rate by 12 to obtain the rate for one month. You should also deduct 10% commission for buying and selling your shares.)

The game is most fun if it is played by several students either in teams or acting as individuals.

Summary of key words and ideas

- Large firms are responsible for an increasing share of total output in the UK. This benefits the firms but may result in certain disadvantages for the consumer.

- Firms are keen to expand because it usually brings greater profits.

- *Diversification* is when firms expand into producing a new range of products or services.

- The *economies of scale* are the benefits gained from producing on a larger scale. The *diseconomies of scale* are the disadvantages of growing larger.

- Firms can expand either by growing themselves or by taking over, or merging with, other companies.

- *Horizontal integration* is when firms at the same stage of production join together. *Vertical integration* is when firms at different stages of production join together — it can be either *forwards* (a firm buys another at a later stage of production) or *backwards* (a firm buys another at an earlier stage of production).

- A *holding company* is one which buys up other companies but keeps the original names of the companies.

- A *public limited company* is a firm which is allowed to sell its shares to the public and is quoted on the Stock Exchange.

- Large firms can raise finance either internally, through the sale of shares, by using profits, by selling assets, or externally through various loans.

- *Debentures* are fixed-interest loans which do not carry voting rights but usually have a prior claim on the assets of the company.

- *Dividend* A dividend is the interest paid on a share. In the case of an ordinary share, it will vary according to how much profit the company makes.

- People buy shares,
  - a to obtain dividends,
  - b to make a capital gain if the price of the share rises,
  - c for the 'perks' which some companies give when shares are purchased,
  - d to influence company policy.

- Companies will use different methods of finance depending upon their requirements.

- The *Stock Exchange* is a market where second-hand shares are bought and sold.

Suggestions for coursework

1 A comparison of four public limited companies. Write to the head offices of public limited companies and ask for copies of company prospectuses, annual reports to shareholders and any other

information they may have available. Compare the companies in terms of,

a what they produce,

b their assets,

c profits and share dividends,

d how they raise their finance — number of shareholders, debenture holders, etc,

e how they have performed in the last year.

2 Trace the shares of any five public limited companies over a period of time. Choose shares in very different types of companies to give a good contrast in performances. Draw graphs to represent the price changes. Compare the graphs of your companies with changes in the Financial Times Index (this is an indication of average share price movements). Which share showed the largest percentage change. (price change/buying price × 100/1)? Can you offer any explanations as to why the shares have changed over the period you have studied them?

Test questions

Atlantic PLC is a holding company with a large number of subsidiaries. It has been particularly successful in the last financial year and has just declared a record dividend on its shares. It is now considering a major expansion of the company which will involve it in several take-over bids. Atlantic hopes that its increasing diversification will result in even higher profits in the future.

1 What do the letters PLC stand for?

2 How is Atlantic different from a private limited company?

3 What are subsidiary companies?

4 What is a dividend on a share?

5 Give two reasons for being a shareholder in Atlantic.

6 What are take-over bids?

7 Why do you think Atlantic wishes to expand?

8 What is meant by 'increasing diversification'?

9 Why might increasing diversification result in higher profits for Atlantic?

10 Suggest four different ways in which Atlantic might finance its expansion. (Include at least one internal and one external method of finance.)

extension questions

RP Knight, a manufacturer of potato crisps, has recently won a contract to supply a major supermarket chain. This has resulted in a doubling of output. The firm has found that their average costs of production have fallen by 2p a packet as a result of the increase in output.

1 Explain how the above illustrates the economies of scale.

2 Give two reasons why doubling output may result in lower average costs.

3 What other benefits might increasing output bring to the firm?

Unit 9   Organising the business

aims   At the end of this unit you should understand:

▶ The need for organisation in firms.

▶ The organisational structure of a large firm.

▶ The function of different departments in a large firm.

▶ The difference between line and staff.

▶ The idea of a chain of command and a span of control.

▶ The advantages and disadvantages of centralised and decentralised systems of organisation.

Why do we need organisation?

case study

Business Report

Hot Dough Bakeries – a rising business

Jean Thomas started Hot Dough Bakeries 10 years ago when she set up her first bakery in a London suburb.

Since then the business has mushroomed and she is now the owner of a chain of 20 shops throughout London.

Jean recalls how 10 years ago she and just one assistant ran that first bakery. This meant ordering supplies, carrying out the actual bread making and baking as well as doing all the paperwork involved in running a small business. Jean's job is very different now. She is no longer seen brushing the flour off her apron or serving customers. She is fully occupied now with the management of her 20 shops. She spends her time in discussions with her bank manager and accountant, appointing managers and developing her business further.

Jean has delegated much of her day-to-day responsibilities to her bakery managers and has also appointed a group of specialists to assist her in the running and expansion of the business. She now employs a Buying Manager to deal with supplies, a Finance Manager to assist with the money side of the business and a Marketing and a Sales Manager to take on responsibility for selling the bakery products.

questions   1 How has Jean's job changed as her business has expanded?

2 Why has Jean needed to change the organisation of her business?

3 Explain what is meant by 'Jean has delegated much of her day-to-day responsibilities'.

4 What other specialist managers might Jean consider employing in the future if the business continues to expand?

How are large businesses organised?

Different businesses have different types of *organisational structure* which vary according to their size, what they do and what the management feels is most appropriate to that particular business. A large manufacturing firm may well have a very different structure from that of a chain of supermarkets.

Talbot Textiles: an example of an organisational structure for a large manufacturing company.

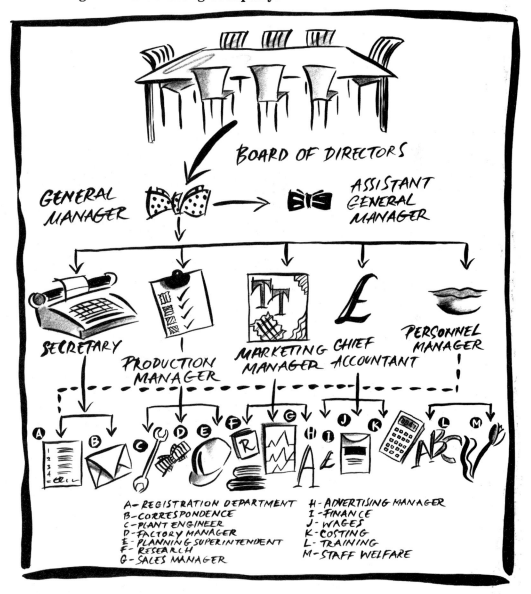

A – REGISTRATION DEPARTMENT
B – CORRESPONDENCE
C – PLANT ENGINEER
D – FACTORY MANAGER
E – PLANNING SUPERINTENDENT
F – RESEARCH
G – SALES MANAGER
H – ADVERTISING MANAGER
I – FINANCE
J – WAGES
K – COSTING
L – TRAINING
M – STAFF WELFARE

exercises

1 Draw an organisation chart for the example of Hot Dough Bakeries on page 104.
2 Draw an organisation chart for your school.

The chain of command

exercise

The chain of command is the way in which orders and instructions are passed down through the organisation from the General Manager to the workers on the shop floor. The order will pass through a number of *levels* (or stages) — rather like the rungs of a ladder.

The General Manager of Talbot Textiles decides to stop all overtime work in the weaving shop from next month.

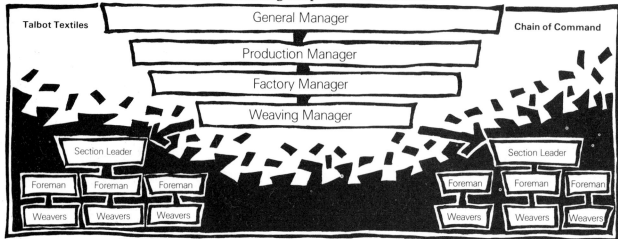

List the people involved in the chain of command in the above decision.

The span of control

The span of control (or the span of responsibility) is the number of people or departments which report to a particular manager. In the case of the Marketing Manager at Talbot Textiles, the span of control is 3.

exercise

1 Draw the chain of command at Talbot Textiles for a decision made by the General Manager to reduce the advertising budget.
2 Draw the chain of command in your school for a decision made by the Head Teacher to reduce the lunch break by 10 minutes in order to end school earlier.
3 What is the span of control of the Chief Accountant at Talbot Textiles?
4 What is the span of control of the Head of Science at your school?

extension questions

1 What problems might arise if the chain of command is very long?
2 It is often said that the span of control of any one manager should not exceed six people. What problems might arise if the span of control were to become greater than six people?

Who does what in a firm?

PROFILE

John MacDonald
Position:
Managing Director

I was appointed to the position of Managing Director by the shareholders of Talbot Textiles. I have overall responsibility for the running of the company and report to the shareholders. I must make sure that the firm conforms to the various rules regarding companies laid down by the Government.

I chair the meetings of the Board of Directors where major decisions are made on company policy. We do not concern ourselves with the day to day running of the company – we have appointed managers to do this for us. It is my job to organise the other directors and make recommendations to the shareholders on such matters as takeovers and merger deals.

PROFILE:

Lynne Partridge
Position:
Company Secretary

After leaving Exeter University with a degree in law, I spent 10 years working in the legal departments of large firms. I joined Talbot Textiles 5 years ago as assistant company secretary and was promoted to my current position last year. I find my legal background very useful as I spend a great deal of my time dealing with such matters as the Company Acts, contracts and patents. I have a small team of legal assistants, clerks and secretaries working for me and I report to the Board of Directors and the General Manager. I work closely with several other departments including accounts, finance and marketing.

PROFILE:

Keith Rae

Position:
Chief Accountant

I joined the financial accounting division of a large engineering firm in Leeds after I qualified as a chartered accountant. I was eventually promoted to finance manager in the same firm. I joined Talbots 10 years ago as assistant chief accountant and took over as chief accountant when my boss retired two years ago.

I am responsible for all finance and accounting which takes place in the firm. My division deals with everything from the accounts for office stationery through to negotiating a £500,000 bank loan. All expenditures and sums of money coming into the firm eventually have to be passed through our books. I need to make sure that any surplus cash we may have is invested wisely. At the same time, I must make sure that the company has sufficient ready cash to meet its current needs.

I report to the finance director and work closely with most other departments in the company. The division is divided into three departments; finance, wages and costing. There is a manager in charge of each of these departments which employ considerable numbers of accountants, clerks and secretaries.

PROFILE:

Sue Rees

Position:
Personnel Manager

I have worked with Talbots ever since leaving school with A levels. The company has always been keen on training and they gave me day release to do a degree in business and management studies at the local polytechnic. I later qualified as a member of the Institute of Personnel Managers.

My job is looking after all matters to do with staff. The personnel department is responsible for the recruiting and selection of staff, training programmes, the health, safety and welfare of all workers, the keeping of employee records and negotiations with the trade unions. There are a considerable number of rules and regulations laid down by the Government concerning the employing of staff, their working conditions and their rights and responsibilities and it is my department's job to make sure they are carried out correctly within the factory.

A key aspect of my job is to do everything possible to improve working relationships and avoid the need for industrial action. With this in mind, I set up a Works Council where representatives from all parts of the firm regularly meet together to discuss problems.

I report to the Board of Directors and to the General Manager on staffing policy and my job inevitably involves a great deal of contact with all other departments within the firm.

PROFILE:

Peter Hall
Position:
Marketing Manager

I joined Talbots five years ago after being marketing manager at a much smaller textile factory in Bradford. The success of Talbots depends upon us being able to sell the finished products to the consumer. That is the work of the marketing departments. If we fail, the whole firm fails – no matter how successful and efficient everyone else is.

As head of the marketing department I am concerned with getting the right products to the right customers. This involves market research to find out what our customers require, advising the research department on product design, advertising and sales promotion as well as ensuring a good distribution service.

We employ an agency to run our advertising campaign for us but it is my job to discuss with them the nature of the campaign and to select from several possible alternative approaches.

I report to the marketing director and have particularly close contact with the production and finance departments.

PROFILE:

Gill Street
Position:
Production Manager

After getting my degree in production engineering at Salford University, I worked in different size engineering firms to gain practical experience. I went back to university to study for a post graduate qualification in management and landed this job after being assistant sales manager at a rival firm. Management has taken me away from actual engineering but my knowledge of what goes on helps me understand the various problems people face on the production side.

The production division is the largest at Talbots and three departmental managers report to me; the plant engineer, who is responsible for the ordering and maintaining of equipment, the factory manager and the planning superintendent, who ensures we have adequate stocks of materials to meet production targets. The division is responsible for all aspects of textile production; spinning, weaving, dyeing and printing. I report direct to the general manager and have to liaise closely with the marketing, personnel and finance departments.

Who deals with this?

exercise For each of the situations given,

a state which department at Talbots you think would be mainly responsible for dealing with it,

b name any other departments you feel might be involved and explain how they would help.

1 The company has just won a major export order to supply a chain of retailers in Denmark. This will mean raising output by overtime working and increasing stocks of raw materials. The Danish importers will be paying one month after final delivery.
2 A rival textile firm has just launched a new line which has taken part of your market for duvet covers. The rival firm is using a new synthetic fibre which is proving to be very popular with customers.
3 Talbots has decided to invest in a new computer-controlled weaving system. The machines for the new system are very expensive and have to be imported from Switzerland.
4 A fall in demand for a particular line has meant the possibility of some redundancies in the spinning shops. The union representing the workers in spinning is resisting any of their members being laid off.

Different types of organisational structure

extension section

- *Line organisation* This is when there are direct lines of responsibility from senior management to the workers on the shop floor. This method of organisation used to be called 'military' because it is how orders are carried out in the army. Employees in a line organisation work solely in one department.

- *Functional organisation* This is where the firm is organised by function — by what people do. The chief accountant, for example, will deal with all departments. Employees who move between departments are called *staff workers*.

- *Line and staff organisations* In reality, most firms have a mixture of both line and staff workers.

Centralised and decentralised organisations

How centralised or decentralised an organisation is depends upon who makes the important decisions. In a very centralised organisation the important decisions are made by management at the centre of the organisation and then passed out as instructions to the various departments. Many major chain stores and supermarkets, such as Boots, Sainsbury and Dixons are highly centralised. Company policy is decided at headquarters, finance is controlled centrally and goods are often bought centrally. Branch managers have very little discretion in the running of individual shops.

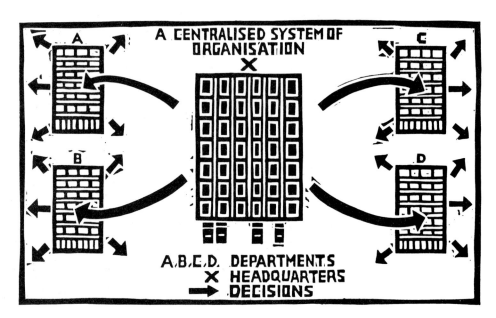

Centralised organisations

Advantages	Disadvantages
Tight control of decisions	Lack of motivation for managers — major decisions taken away from them
Decisions made by experts	Central management may lack knowledge of local conditions
Achieve uniformity throughout the organisation	Central management may lack contact with 'shop floor'
Avoids repetition of functions — allows bulk buying	May be slow to react to changes

Centralised organisations tend to be those where the firm is dealing with the same or very similar products or services throughout, such as chains of shops, banks and fast food restaurants, where the customer expects the same service or provision of goods throughout the UK.

a What types of decisions will divisions A, B, C, D be allowed to make?

b What information will X require from A, B, C, D?

c How will A, B, C, D communicate with X and with each other?

Decentralised organisations

Decentralised organisations delegate many important decisions to managers of divisions and departments. In decentralised organisations managers are given a great deal of freedom to make the decisions they feel are best for their part of the organisation. The central management will only make the really major decisions but will otherwise allow the various divisions and departments to function independently. Examples of very decentralised organisations include Lonhro, Dunlop and ICI.

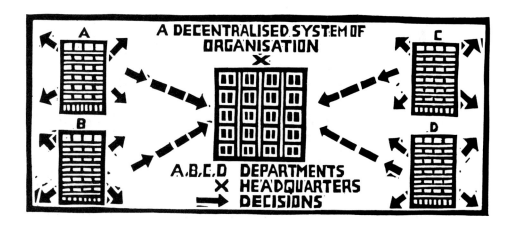

Advantages	Disadvantages
Increases motivation of managers	Managers may lack sufficient expertise — wrong decisions may be made
Department managers may have better understanding of what is required in their area	Local decisions may run counter to policy required by the company
Decisions may be made quicker because less consultation needed	Firm may fail to benefit from the economies of scale, such as bulk buying

Decentralised organisations tend to be those where there is little relationship between the various divisions in the company. This is the case with holding companies that own a number of firms producing very different products and services.

Summary of key words and ideas

- The need for a proper organisational structure increases as the business grows larger.
- *Delegate responsibility* To give authority to others to make decisions on matters previously dealt with by a more senior person in the organisation.
- As an organisation expands, the need for delegation of responsibilities and decision making increases.
- *The chain of command* The way in which decisions are passed down an organisation.
- *Span of control* The number of people or departments reporting to a manager.
- *Line organisation* Employees work in one department and decisions are passed down the organisation in a direct line from senior management to shop floor workers.
- *Functional organisation* Where the firm is organised on the basis of what people do.
- *Staff workers* Employees who move between various departments in their job.
- *Centralised organisation* Where the organisation is tightly controlled from the centre and there is little delegation of responsibility.
- *Decentralised organisation* Where divisions or departments in the firm are given powers to take major decisions.

Suggestions for coursework

1 Draw an organisation chart for any organisation you are familiar with, such as school, a club, sports centre, youth club, etc. Use your chart to illustrate the terms 'chain of command' and 'span of control'. Find out the exact responsibilities of any four people in the organisation and list them.

2 Compare the organisation of any two contrasting firms (large/small, manufacturing/service, etc.) How is responsibility delegated? What are the chains of command in the two firms? Why are the firms differently organised? Compare the responsibilities of two managers in each of the organisations.

3 A 'mini-enterprise' activity taking place in school or college could be used to look at organisational structures. How was the business organised? Was this developed by the group or imposed by someone else? How did it work in practice? Who did what? What problems were there in terms of the organisation? How much work was delegated — how much was centralised?

Test questions

JK Whittaker Ltd is a medium-sized firm making marine engines. The company is organised into five main departments: production, marketing, finance, personnel and distribution. The production department is further divided into three sections: research and development, assembly, and plant maintenance.

The Chairman of the Board of Directors has recently instructed the General Manager to inform all departmental managers of the need to reduce expenditure by 5% in order to meet financial targets in the coming year.

1 Construct an organisational chart for Whittakers from the information contained in the above passage.
2 Briefly explain the type of work you would expect to be carried out by:
   a The production department,
   b the marketing department and,
   c the personnel department.
3 What is the Board of Directors? What types of decisions will it be responsible for?
4 What work is done by a Departmental Manager?
5 What is the span of control at Whittakers of
   a the General Manager,
   b the Production Manager?
6 What is the chain of command for carrying out the order to reduce spending by 5%?
7 It is decided to subdivide the marketing department into three sections. Suggest an appropriate way of dividing it up.
8 Which department manager would each of the following be mainly responsible to:
   a a delivery driver,
   b a salesman,
   c a toolmaker,
   d the staff training officer,
   e an accounts clerk?

Extension questions

1 Whittakers, like most organisations, has both line and staff workers. Explain the terms 'line' and 'staff', giving an example of each from Whittakers.
2 Whittakers has a centralised system of personnel record keeping but a decentralised system of accounting. Explain the terms 'centralised' and 'decentralised' as used in this context and discuss the advantages and disadvantages of the two methods of organisation as they are used here.

Unit 10 Communicating

aims At the end of this unit you should understand:

▶ The need for good communications in business.
▶ The range of different types of internal and external communications.
▶ The suitability of particular forms of communication.
▶ How communications can be improved and made more efficient.
▶ How information is stored and retrieved in business.

The need for good communications in business

Communication is the passing of information between people. Good communications are essential for the efficient functioning of a business. These communications may range from informal conversations to the most sophisticated electronic forms of communications available.

exercise

An urgent order has just come into your firm and you need to pass the details on to the production manager who is in the next building.

1 List all the possible ways of getting the information to the production manager.
2 What might happen if you do not get the information to the production manager quickly and accurately?
3 Which method of communication would you choose in this case?

Types of communications

Communications can be divided into two groups: *internal* (communications used within the firm) and *external* (communicating with people outside the firm). There is some overlap between the two groups — the telephone, for example, is used both for communicating within the firm and with people outside it. At the same time, some companies may be on many different sites which are spread throughout the country.

Internal communications

Internal telephone

+ Fast, avoids the need to move around.

− Conversations not normally recorded. No record of information. Verbal messages may be misunderstood.

Face-to-face contact

May be informal 'chats' or formal meetings where details are recorded in the 'minutes'.

+ May sort out problems more rapidly and avoid unnecessary paper work.

− People not always available for meetings. Often no record kept and information may be misinterpreted.

Internal memo

Short, hand-written or typed note giving information.

+ Record kept of information sent out. Less open to misinterpretation than verbal messages.

− May come to be disregarded if over-used.

Formal report

Long document giving details of for example a particular meeting or company policy. May be copied or circulated between staff.

+ Provides an accurate and detailed record of the information.

− Can involve a great deal of paper circulating in the firm. Reports may not be read if too long and the staff are short of time. Vital information may be lost in the details of the report if it is not summarised.

Noticeboards

Used to display notices concerning large groups of people.

+ Can be eye catching — use of colour, pictures, etc. Saves on copying.

− May not be seen. Needs to be kept up-to-date. No good for confidential documents.

Computer terminals

Departments linked together by computer. Departments can both input and receive information.

+ Fast means of communicating. Suitable for both short messages and long reports. Departments can select the information required.

− Initially expensive to install. Lack of confidentiality.

Company magazine/newsletter

Normally a feature of large companies. Used for general information on how the company is performing, social activities, changes of personnel, etc.

+ Helps to give company a feeling of unity. Assists employees to see what is going on in the whole organisation.

− Costly to produce — needs editing, printing, etc. No guarantee it will be read.

Cordless telephones/radio paging

Employees who move around a great deal in the firm may be contacted by 'bleeper' — they then go to the nearest telephone extension.

+ Cordless telephones allow employees to speak from wherever they are.

− Expensive if used for large numbers of employees.

Dictaphone messages

Tape-recorded information. Letters can be recorded whilst awaiting typing. Messages can be left for staff temporarily out of the office.

+ May mean more efficient use of secretarial staff by having a 'pool' of typists.

− Messages easily misunderstood. Training needed in accurate and clear dictation of letters. Need for audio-typists.

Choosing the best way of communicating

1 For each of the following situations, suggest three possible ways of communicating the information. Choose the way you feel is best and say why you have selected this particular method.
   a The Managing Director wishes to call a meeting of all Departmental Managers in two weeks' time.
   b The Marketing Manager wishes to have a letter typed but her secretary is out at lunch and she has to go to an important meeting before the secretary is likely to return.
   c The Production Manager urgently requires details of an order from the Despatch Department which is located some distance from his office.
   d The Personnel Manager wishes to inform all staff of the arrangements for the Christmas Party.
   e One of the secretaries in the Marketing Department wishes to arrange special leave to look after a sick relative.
2 Prepare a notice on A4 paper for the staff noticeboard announcing the formation of a social club in the firm. Make your notice as eye-catching as possible and include all relevant information, such as when it meets, what activities are on offer, the names of the organisers, etc.
3 Write a memo from the Distribution Manager to Ms J Roberts in the packing department, asking her to ensure that all orders for PR Supplies Ltd are completed by the end of the month.

The Rules For Good Communication

1 Keep it as simple as possible. Think about what you really want to say and avoid information which is unnecessary or irrelevant.
2 Be accurate. The message must be understood in the way you intend it. People respond differently to spoken and written words.
3 Choose the most appropriate form of communication – an informal chat may be more effective than a formal letter.
4 Think of your audience. Who is the message intended for? Different styles of communication are required for friends, customers and managing directors.
5 Be clear about what you expect to happen as a result of the communication. Do you expect an immediate response? Is it something to discuss further? Is the message for information or is it trying to influence someone in their thinking?
6 Timing of the communication. There may be some times which are more appropriate than others. A busy executive may not wish to engage in a lengthy discussion five minutes before an important meeting.

External communications

The post

- Despite many advances in communications, the postal system is still very heavily used by nearly all firms. Examples of common use include: the sending of documents such as orders and invoices; sending advertising information to possible customers; sending letters to suppliers, customers and other firms.
- The postal system is a relatively cheap and safe way of sending written information.
- The main disadvantage of the postal system is that it is relatively slow. The Post Office is trying to speed up the sorting and delivery of letters by using an electronic system based on the post code on the letter. There are also some special postal services which are quicker than the normal letter delivery but which cost considerably more than ordinary letters.

Special delivery

Guarantees delivery of letters and parcels the next day. Letters arriving at their destination after the postman has left will be delivered by messenger.

Express delivery

Provides a special service for the delivery of letters to the Channel Islands, Isle of Man and Republic of Ireland.

Datapost Sameday

Offers a sameday service for letters and parcels between and within major business centres in the UK.

Datapost Overnight

Guarantees next-day courier delivery for urgent goods and documents. Delivery takes palce before noon the next day to most of the UK.

Red Star

A service run by British Rail. Packages are handed in at certain railway stations and sent by the next passenger train to their destination.

Other Post Office services

Registered post

A safer way of sending valuable items or documents through the post. A signature is obtained upon delivery of the item. The sender is compensated if the item is lost or stolen.

Recorded delivery

The service is cheaper than registered post and provides proof of posting. Only a small amount of compensation is paid if the item is lost or stolen, so it is not suitable for valuables. It is useful in sending such items as bills, and final demands for payment, as evidence that they were posted and received.

Poste restante

Letters and packets can be sent to a post office in a particular town for collection. This is useful for sales representatives who may be uncertain where they will be staying during a sales tour.

Certificate of posting

This is a free service which shows the date of posting. This may provide useful evidence in business in the event of a dispute.

Freepost

This allows customers to write back to a business free of charge. This encourages people to respond to advertisements and enquire for further details. A similar system is the Business Reply service where customers are provided with special pre-printed envelopes to reply free of charge. In both cases the form offering Freepost or Business Reply services pays the cost of the postage.

The telephone

The telephone remains one of the most important forms of external communication. It is a rapid and relatively cheap form of verbal communication. The cost of using it depends upon the time of day (it is most expensive in the mornings during working days), the length of the call, and the distance. Most places throughout the world can be reached by direct dialling without using an operator.

Equipment such as Answerphones and extensions can either be rented or bought from British Telecom or approved companies. There remains a charge for the rental of telephone lines — the more outside lines a firm has, the greater the charge. Most large firms have a private exchange (*PABX*) operated by a telephonist which enables outside calls to be connected to particular extensions within the firm. Employees who travel a great deal can maintain contact with the firm by having radio telephones installed in their cars.

```
11/10/88 12:03
Telex line 1 - Message RE7825    received at 11/10/88 12:02

837330 OXPRES G
TLX.REF:92,8  88-10-11  12:02


34313  OXPRES G

ATTN : ALISON PRIOR
----------------------
PLEASE FIND OUR QUOTATION FOR YOUR NEXT COMPUTER SYSTEM.
I TRUST THAT IT INCLUDES ALL THE ITEMS WE DISCUSSED.

PLEASE NOTE THAT TANDON OFFER A SIX MONTH WARRANTY FOR ALL THEIR
COMPUTER EQUIPMENT.

I HOPE THIS CLARIFIES EVERYTHING TO YOUR SATISFACTION.

REGARDS
J.JONES.
OXFORD UNIVERSITY PRESS. CORBY U.K+
837330 OXPRES G
34313  OXPRES G
```

Telex

This allows firms to communicate directly with other companies either within the UK or abroad. Firms having this facility are given a Telex number. The firm sending the information dials the firm it wishes to contact and then types the message on a teleprinter. The information is received through the telephone lines and printed out by the firm's telex machine.

The Telex system is not only very rapid but also gives written confirmation of information. Telex messages can be used as legal contracts. Provided the Telex machine is left on, information can be received from other firms 24-hours a day. This is particularly useful when dealing with countries that are on very different time to the UK. Telex users rent teleprinters and the cost of sending a message depends upon the distance it is being sent and the length of the message. Telex numbers are listed in the Telex Directory.

Telemessage

Businesses can send a message by telephone or telex to a Post Office sorting office for delivery with the next day's first class post.

Bureaufax (Often shortened to Fax)

A fax machine

This is an increasingly popular method of sending black-and-white printed material or drawings very rapidly between two firms. The information on A4 paper is copied and sent electronically between two Fax machines using the telephone lines. The cost of sending the message depends upon the distance between the two firms and the length of time it takes to transmit the information.

Confravision

To save managers travelling long distances for meetings, they can go to their nearest Confravision studio and be linked by sound and vision to managers elsewhere in the country.

Telegrams

Not all overseas firms have a Telex facility and telegrams are still sometimes used for sending short, urgent written messages abroad. (There is no internal telegram service now.) The cost of the telegram is determined by the number of words in the message and the place it is being sent to. To reduce the cost, firms try and cut down the length of the message as much as possible while still making sure it is accurate.

Computerised information systems

In the past few years there has been a very rapid growth in a variety of computerised information systems.

Prestel

Prestel is the British Telecom information system. Firms connected to Prestel can receive information on a wide range of topics such as Stock Exchange prices, financial reports, and travel information. The system also allows users to request particular pieces of information and to make bookings for items such as airline tickets.

Ceefax and Oracle services are provided by the broadcasting authorities and are similar to Prestel but they do not allow users to input information in the same way.

Electronic mailing

Electronic mailing systems, such as Times Network and Datel, allow firms both to receive and input information. The information is received through a computer terminal linked to the telephone system by a *modem*. Each firm involved in the system has a *post box number* to which information can be sent.

Electronic mailing systems are very useful to firms spread over a number of different sites and requiring frequent contacts to be made between the various offices. It also allows a head office to maintain centralised control over its branches. (see Unit 9)

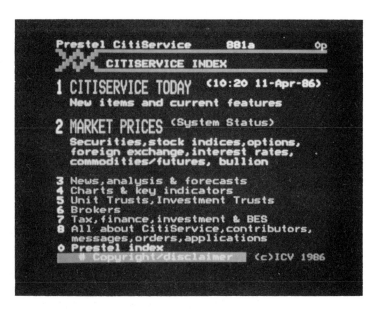

City news displayed on a Prestel screen

exercises

1 You receive the following Telex message;

```
23/9/87
GLM SPARES LTD
WEMBLEY, MIDDX.


FAO MRS D SMITH, DESPATCH DEPT.

REF. ORDER NO. 1987B/104 DTD, 30/6/87.   PLEASE
ARRANGE URGENT DESPATCH BY AIR FREIGHT.   VITAL
THAT GOODS RECEIVED BY 5/10/87.


REGARDS
S JONES, PURCHASING DEPT.
BELL INTERNATIONAL COMMUNICATIONS,
3125 HAVARD ST. BOSTON, MASS. USA

837330 OXPRES G
34313  OXPRES G
```

a Write the same information out in the form of a business letter.

b Write a Telex message back to Bell International Communications
confirming that you have despatched the items on flight number
BA/3085, due to arrive at Logan Airport, Boston at 5pm, local
time on 5th October 1987.

c Using the Post Office Guide, calculate the cost of sending your
message.

d How much, approximately, would it have cost to have sent the
same information, i) by telephone, ii) by telegram?

2 For each of the following situations choose the most appropriate form
of communication and say why you feel that this would be the best in
the circumstances:

a The head office of a supermarket chain wishes to communicate
regular price changes to its branch stores.

b A firm in London needs to send an important contract to a firm in
Birmingham to arrive the following day.

c A firm in Newcastle wishes to contact its agent who is currently in
a small town in Kenya.

d A marketing manager in York wishes to discuss a proposal with an
advertising agency in London.

e An investment trust in Norwich wishes to obtain regular
information on share prices and interest rates.

f A firm in Manchester wishes to send a written estimate to a firm in
Cardiff the same day.

Storing and retrieving information

So far in this unit we have been concerned with the ways in which information is passed between people. Businesses also have to store information and be able to refer to parts of it when it is required in the future. For example, firms need to store information on their clients, keep copies of invoices and customer records, and to retain copies of contracts and other legal documents. The storing, classification and retrieving of information is called *information technology*. Firms may have systems ranging from simple filing cabinets through to the most up-to-date computerised data storage.

Electronic data storage is becoming increasingly important as the amount of information to be stored grows. Computerised systems have the advantage of being able to store very large amounts of information on disk or tape and this can be 'found' very rapidly. Information recorded on a spreadsheet, or in a database can be rearranged and extracted in a variety of ways to suit the user. This is illustrated in the case study on Direct Fashions Ltd on the next page.

Where large quantities of information change frequently, such as stock prices, a firm's records can be updated by receiving a computer disk or tape with the alterations on. This information is then very rapidly fed into the firm's computer.

Whatever system of storage is used, the firm needs to decide upon a method of organising the information. A filing system can be organised in a variety of ways — by name of subject, by date, by account number, etc. The method chosen will depend upon the type of information being stored and the way in which it needs to be most frequently retrieved.

Direct Fashions Ltd

Direct Fashions is a mail-order clothing firm. It has a large number of customers throughout the UK and uses a computer system for storing information about them. Apart from keeping details of the customer's account, Direct Fashions records a great deal of information about each of the customers. The computer is able to give information on what each customer has bought, their age, social class, their tastes in clothes and what their *spending power* is likely to be. This information is of great value to the marketing manager who can construct *profiles* of the company's customers. When a new range of fashions comes in she can quickly extract information from the computer as to which customers are likely to be most interested in it. This saves time and money sending advertising to customers whose profiles indicate that they are very unlikely to buy the new fashion range. From the company's database the marketing manager could, for example, obtain a list of all customers in the age range 35–45 who have previously bought knitted items from Direct Fashions.

questions

1 What advantages are there for Direct Fashions of using a computerised system of storing customer information?
2 What is meant by a customer profile?
3 Imagine that you are a customer of Direct Fashions. Draw up a computer print-out of the information Direct Fashions might have on you.

example

```
NAME              Philip Spencer
ACCOUNT NO.       PS/3456/82
ADDRESS           21, The Rise, East Bainbridge, Notts.
AGE               27
DATE OF FIRST PURCHASE    2-4-82
DATE OF LAST PURCHASE     5-9-87
```

Communication problems

How poor communications cost Spender Bros £20 000.

Spender Bros, a firm making electrical components, were contacted by telephone for an urgent quotation to supply Trend Electronics with a large quantity of specialised switches. The telephonist transferred the call to the sales manager. The sales manager was at a meeting and her secretary was out at lunch. The caller from Trend Electronics was left hanging on for five minutes before being told that there was nobody available to take the call. The caller left a message with the telephonist asking the sales manager to telephone him as soon as possible. The telephonist forgot to inform the sales manager of the call from Trend Electronics until the next day.

The following day the sales manager telephoned Trend Electronics and jotted the details of the request for a quotation down. She passed these on to the production manager later the same day. Unfortunately, the production manager was not told that the matter was urgent and did nothing about it for three days. Trend Electronics again contacted the sales manager at Spender Bros to remind her about the quotation. The sales manager contacted the production manager who had now lost the original piece of paper with the details on it. The sales manager had not made a copy of the order but thought she could remember the details. Unfortunately, the sales manager got the type of switch wrong.

The quotation finally arrived at Trend Electronics late and incorrect. Not surprisingly, Spender Bros did not get the contract and lost £20 000 worth of business.

exercise List all the mistakes which were made in communications by Spender Bros and suggest how the matter should have been properly dealt with, starting from the initial telephone call from Trend Electronics.

Communication nets

One problem often faced by large firms is a lack of understanding by any one section of the company as to what the other sections are doing. This was one of the *diseconomies of scale* mentioned in Unit 8.

It is very important that information within the organisation is received by all those that it may have an effect upon. A very common complaint in large organisations is that workers on the factory floor are not informed of decisions made by management until it actually starts to influence working conditions. This has frequently been a cause of industrial action. This is dealt with in detail in Unit 13.

exercise How information is passed around in an organisation is very important for the efficient running of the firm. Here are several different types of *communication nets* which show who communicates with who in an organisation. For each one,
  a describe how it operates and,
  b say what you think the advantages and disadvantages of the particular method are, eg, Who receives the information? How rapid is the system? Who does it involve in decision making?

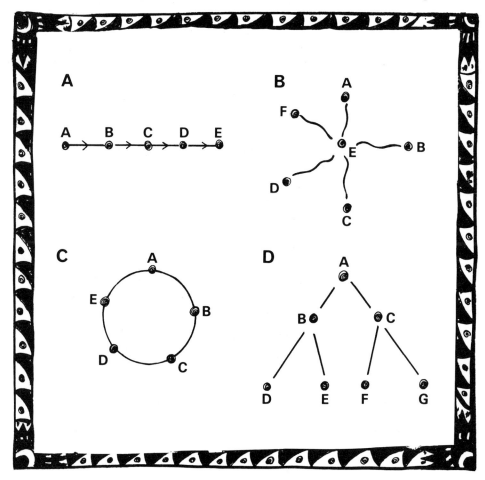

Summary of key words and ideas

- As firms expand the need for a *system of communications* increases.
- *Good communications* are vital for the efficient running of a firm. Poor communications can lead to loss of business and poor relationships between various parts of the workforce.
- *Internal communications* are those taking place within the firm and include: face-to-face contacts, telephones, memos, reports, noticeboards, computer terminals, newsletters and dictaphones.
- *External communications* are when a firm communicates with those outside the organisation and include: post, telephone, Telex, telegrams, electronic mailing and information systems.
- Different types of information are suited to particular methods of communication depending upon their nature, the speed with which they need to be received and whether they are best presented in written or verbal form.
- *Information technology* is the classification, storage and retrieval of information.
- Electronic systems of storing information are becoming increasingly important in organisations. They can store large quantities of information in a small area and can reorganise information to best suit the purpose of the user.
- *Communications nets* are the patterns of how communications are organised in a firm.

Suggestions for coursework

1 Invent a firm and describe what methods of internal and external communications are used. Give precise examples of how the various methods of communications would be used. Draw diagrams to show how different departments communicate with each other.

2 Carry out the above task with a real firm. The task could be further improved by making a comparison of two different organisations.

3 Using data from the Post Office Guide and from British Telecom, do a comparison of the cost and speed of sending a variety of types of information by different methods of communication.

4 Develop either a paper (manual) or electronic file for an estate agent. Store information,
   a by customer requirements,
   b by types of property for sale.
   Explain how you have organised your information.

Test questions

1 JM Martyn Ltd are a large firm producing office equipment. They sell their products mainly in the UK but import some materials from West Germany.
   a Name four forms of internal communication the firm would use. Give a specific example of how the firm would use each method of communication.
   b Name four types of external communication the firm would use. Include two methods of communication that the firm would use for its dealings with West Germany. Give an example of the use of each method chosen.
2 You have recently taken up a post with the Easiway Travel Agency. They have purchased a computer which is linked up to the major travel companies and is also used for storing information on their customers.
   a Explain how their computer link with the travel companies would be used.
   b List the types of information Easiway might hold on each customer.
   c Suggest two other uses that Easiway might make of the computer.
3 Explain the use a large manufacturing company might make of the following forms of communication:
   a Telex,
   b Datapost,
   c Confravision,
   d Bureaufax.
4 A large estate agents has several different ways of filing information. One method it uses is to file alphabetically according to the name of the customer. Suggest two other methods of filing the estate agent might make use of. In each case explain how the system would work and what use it would be to the estate agent.

Extension questions

1 The marketing department in a large manufacturing firm feels that the finance department too frequently fails to communicate important information. Suggest two ways in which communications could be improved between the marketing and finance departments.
2 Draw two different types of communication nets. For each net chosen suggest,
   a the type of information it would be used for,
   b its advantages and disadvantages for communicating information.

Unit 11   Production

aims   At the end of this unit you should understand:

▶   The factors influencing the location of a firm.

▶   The different methods of producing a product.

▶   The flow of production.

▶   The division of labour.

▶   The impact of changing technology on production.

Locating the enterprise

Where shall we put our firm? There are a large number of factors which may influence where a firm is located. A great deal depends upon what the firm is producing. A firm involved in writing computer programs may well be able to locate almost anywhere in the country, while a heavy engineering firm will be much more limited in its location.

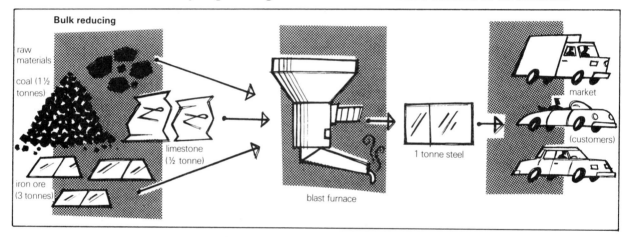

Materials versus markets

Some firms tend to locate close to where their materials are available. This may be close to the source of the materials, such as mines, quarries, forests, etc, or where the firm can obtain easy access to materials by being close to ports, major roads and rail links.

Firms locating close to raw materials, or where there is easy access to them, are often *bulk reducing* industries. This means that the product being produced is lighter, or less bulky, than the raw materials needed to make it. It is therefore cheaper to make the product as close as possible to the raw materials rather than pay high transport costs to move the materials to a factory some distance away. A good example of this is the steel industry. It takes 5 tonnes of materials to produce 1 tonne of steel. Early steel works tended to be located on those coalfields which also had iron ore and limestone. More recent steel works, using imported iron ore, tend to be located near to ports which also have easy access to coal.

Other firms which tend to be located close to the source of raw materials include those dealing in perishable items, such as fish canning and vegetable freezing.

The pull of the market

Firms which are *bulk increasing* tend to be located close to the market for their products. Bulk increasing means that the good being produced is larger or heavier than the materials being used to make it. Examples of such industries include firms making boxes for packing, soft drink manufacturers and baking. It is clearly cheaper to transport the raw materials to the market than move the more bulky finished good.

Other industries which normally locate close to their market include services, such as banking and finance, where close contact with customers is important. Perishable foods which cannot be processed, such as lettuces, are also often produced close to their markets — although improvements in transport and growing methods have meant that they can now be grown further from their market.

Other factors influencing location

Planning permission

Firms normally require planning permission from the local authority in order to set up a new factory. Certain areas will often be designated for industrial development while restrictions may be placed on developments close to housing or in rural areas.

Site facilities

Some manufacturing firms require large, flat sites and may have particular needs, such as a gas supply, special waste disposal facilities and a good water supply.

Transport facilities

Many manufacturing firms need good transport facilities in order to obtain materials and components and to move the finished products to the customer. Because of congestion, many firms have moved out of towns and cities and have located close to motorways outside of urban areas. Major airports have also attracted firms which have close connections with other countries.

Skilled labour

Some industries rely on particular types of skilled workers. Certain areas develop a reputation for possessing specialist skills. A recent example of this has been the growth of high-tech industries around Cambridge, partly based on the skills and research facilities available at the university there.

Historical factors

Sometimes the reasons for an industry developing in the past in a particular location have disappeared and yet the industry remains there because it is well established in the area and because the costs of moving are high. This is known as *industrial inertia*. An example of this is the Cumbria pencil industry, which was originally based upon local supplies of graphite but which now uses synthetic materials.

Government influence

We have seen in Unit 5 how government and local authorities have attempted to attract industry to areas of high unemployment by offering them grants and other incentives. This has certainly influenced the location of at least some firms. A recent example has been the locating of the Nissan car factory near Sunderland in the north-east of England.

Linkages

Some firms are very dependent upon others. They may supply components to a large firm or deal in the by-products of other firms. (A by-product is something produced in the making of another product.) Other firms, particularly those providing services, often need to be in close personal contact with similar types of organisations. This can be seen in the City of London where there is a tremendous concentration of financial businesses close to the Bank of England and the Stock Exchange.

The Bank of England

TYNESIDE ENTERPRISE ZONE

GETS YOU GOING.

ENTERPRISE ZONE BENEFITS

A stimulating freedom from general rates, Development Land Tax and red tape, plus 100% allowance against taxes on building costs...

The Stock Exchange

Location

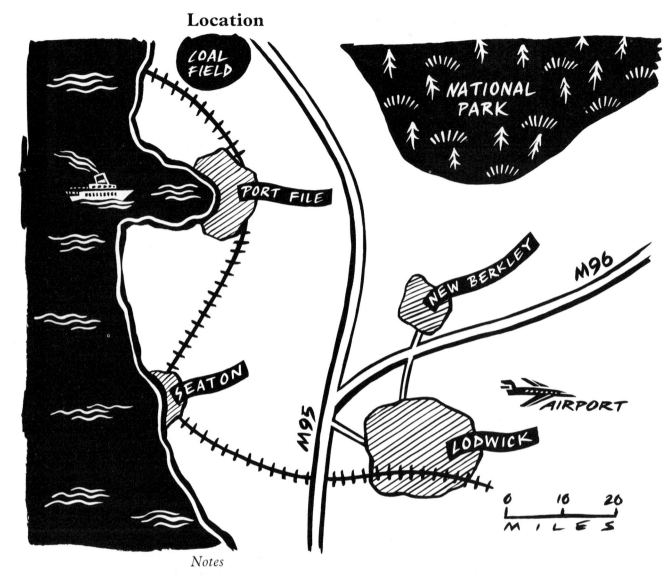

Notes

Lodwick is the main town in the area with a population of 500 000 residents. It is a centre for trade and commerce and has excellent shopping facilities which serve the town and the surrounding area.

New Berkley — a new town development with a population of 50 000. There is local authority assistance for firms locating there. It has several industrial estates and there is a range of modern factory accommodation.

Port File has a population of 120 000. It has a harbour which will accommodate large ocean-going ships. There is a small fishing fleet based in the west of the town and a number of industries connected with the town's function as a port.

Seaton — a popular holiday resort as well as a retirement town. It has a population of 30 000. There is a range of holiday accommodation and a small shopping centre.

exercises

1 For each of the following firms choose the best location in the area shown on the map opposite, giving your reasons for each decision:
   a A steelworks.
   b A firm concerned with freezing and processing fresh fish.
   c A light engineering firm requiring a large, flat site and good road communications to obtain its components and to transport its finished products.
   d A firm offering a range of personal financial services.
   e A DIY hypermarket.
   f A craft shop.

2 A firm producing chemicals wishes to locate in the area shown on the map. They are informed by the local authority that there are three areas where they will not be allowed to locate.
   a Which three locations do you think they are referring to and why?
   b Where do you think the best location would be for the chemical works?

3 Suggest types of firms, apart from those already mentioned, which might be found in:
   a Port File,
   b Seaton,
   c New Berkley,
   d Lodwick,
   and say why you feel that they would be located there.

4 **a** Why are the firms pictured below located where they are?
   b For any one of these firms, say how the factors influencing its location have changed in the past 30 years.

A data handling service

An oil refinery

A steel works

Organising production

There are three types of production organisation: Job, Batch and Flow.

Job production
This is when a firm gets one-off orders so that each product is built to the customer's specifications. This type of work is often done by relatively small, specialist firms. It is difficult in this type of production to have a flow line (see below).

JC Buchanan Ltd are specialists in ocean-going yachts. Each yacht is built to the customer's requirements, which means that no two yachts are ever identical. The workers at Buchanan's tend to work as a team and there is little specialisation in the production of each yacht.

Job production

Batch production

Batch production lies between job and flow production. A clothing manufacturer, for example, may receive *batch* orders for 1000 particular skirts. The firm can set up a production line for this type of work because it involves some repetition of particular tasks. After the batch is produced it will switch to something else.

Flow production (mass production)

Flow production is used when firms receive very large orders for identical products. Cars, canned foods, electrical goods and sweets are all normally produced by flow production. This involves using assembly lines where each worker does a small task and repeats it over and over again. This is called the *division of labour* and is used in *mass production*.

Flow production

The flow of production

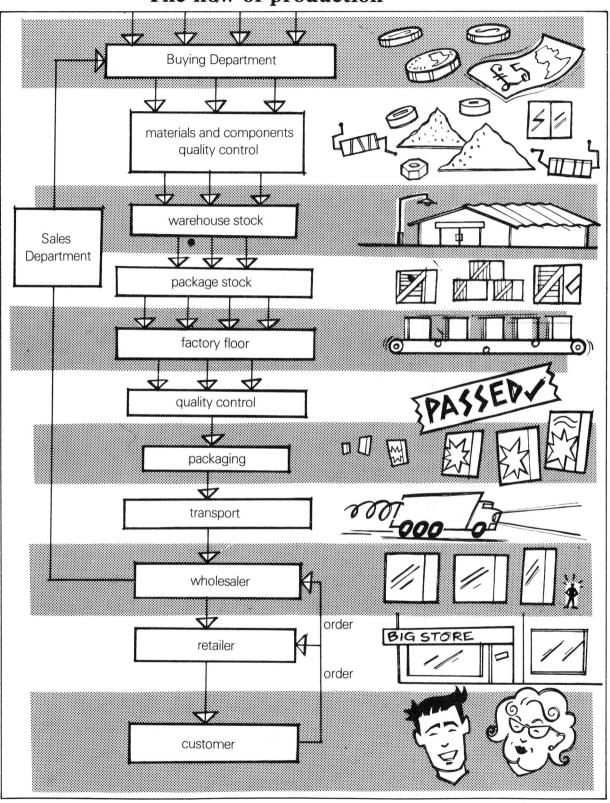

Specialisation and the division of labour

Modern mass production methods normally require a considerable degree of specialisation by the workforce. Each worker carries out a small part of the total assembly, often alongside a conveyer belt which brings the components to each worker. It is argued that the division of labour results in higher *productivity* (the amount each worker produces in an hour) and that this leads to lower average costs of production. This is because:

- Each task is very simple, so workers get very quick at carrying it out.
- Little training is required to learn each task.
- Workers can be allocated to the tasks they are best at.
- Workers may find better ways of carrying out a particular task.
- Machines are in constant use.
- Use of assembly-line methods with less time wasted moving around the factory.

The division of labour may however have disadvantages. some of these are illustrated by the following case study.

---

case study

A life in the day of Winston Graham, car worker

'I am on the day shift today which means clocking in at 8·30 am. I'm working in the engine assembly plant fitting pistons. I've been doing this for the past ten shifts. You get moved around every three weeks but it still gets pretty boring. You can learn how to do most of the jobs in ten minutes and you start getting bored after the first hour. I can fit pistons now without even thinking about it. As soon as the belt starts up I let my mind wander — its the only way to stay sane, and it helps to pass the time. I think about where I'm going on my holidays next month, what's an TV tonight or about the girl I met at the Club last Saturday — my mind's on anything except the job I'm doing. Sometimes I make a mistake because I'm not thinking about what I'm doing and back the block comes from Quality Control.

Every two hours we get a twenty-minute break. It's so far to go to the canteen that they bring food and drinks round on a trolley now. I can't say I get much satisfaction from this job — apart from the money at the end of the week. There's not much to talk about when I go home after the shift.

This afternoon we got an unofficial break. Something went wrong down the line which brought all of us to a standstill. I've thought about changing jobs a few times — I couldn't stick this for the rest of my life. The problem is, jobs are not easy to come by these days and this one doesn't exactly give you much of a training for anything else.'

questions

1 What disadvantages of the division of labour are illustrated by the case study opposite?
2 What satisfaction did Winston get from his job? How would this compare to the satisfaction a cabinet maker would get from his job?
3 What improvements could be made at the car factory to help to overcome some of the disadvantages of the division of labour?

Improving assembly line work

- One of the main disadvantages of the division of labour is that the workers fail to gain satisfaction from the job and this leads to boredom and consequently poor standards of output. It is also claimed that this is one cause of strike action and loss of production. Workers are made to feel that they are 'a very small cog in a large wheel' and this results in them not having an interest in the product as a whole: they feel *alienated*.

- Some firms have tried to overcome these problems by:

  1 Moving workers between jobs more frequently.
  2 Giving workers more involved and interesting tasks to do.
  3 Having groups of workers make a particular section of the product.
  4 Offering bonuses and other incentives. (See Unit 12.)
  5 Making the working conditions more interesting — playing music, having a factory radio station, etc.

- The Volvo car company in Sweden used some of these methods and found that the quality of their cars increased and fewer were rejected because of faults. Productivity increased compared with when they had a very intensive division of labour.

case study   People in production

The following people all have jobs in production at a factory making and assembling washing machines. Here they briefly describe their jobs and how modern technology has changed the nature of production.

Jean Render, Factory Manager

'I was the only woman to graduate in mechanical engineering in my year at polytechnic and it is still unusual for a woman to be a factory manager. I am responsible for everything that happens — or fails to happen — in my factory. I am also responsible for the factory itself. I lead a team of specialists. I did several of their jobs before becoming manager and my knowledge has proved very useful.

Modern technology has had a big impact on our company in the last few years. Machines have replaced many workers and we are now producing more washing machines with a much smaller workforce than ten years ago. I can see more jobs disappearing from the factory floor in the next few years too. It's a great pity to see the decline in jobs but we have to remain competitive.'

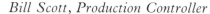

Bill Scott, Production Controller

'Everything produced in the factory is done according to a plan and it is my job to see that everything runs smoothly. I need to make sure that we have enough of the correct materials in stock in order to meet production targets, that there are no unnecessary holdups in the production flow and that things get done on time. Hiccups in production may mean a loss of revenue if we are unable to meet our orders.

I said that everything is produced according to a plan and this is being increasingly done by computer technology. Computers assist greatly in stock control and help to achieve a smooth flow of materials through the factory. The computers can also pinpoint very quickly where any problem is occurring in production. This has meant a lot of retraining for me but it has made my job more interesting.'

June Lemont, Quality Control Inspector

'I have been working here since I left school. I started on the shop floor as a machine operator and worked my way up to this position. Gaining promotion meant getting some training and qualifications and the firm was very good in allowing me day-release to go to the local technical college and then to polytechnic. My job is to make sure that what is being produced comes up to the correct standards — what's laid down in the specifications. This means checking quality at every stage in production — from the materials through to the finished machine.

Every year we use more sophisticated methods of quality control in order to improve the reliability of our products. We used to check everything by hand using gauges and scales or by just looking at it. These days a lot of that is done by machines linked to computers. They can tell straight away if a part is the minutest amount out from the specifications. We used to check the quality of the paintwork by eye, that's now done by lasers which can tell the thickness and level of the paint. All this has changed my job and those of the people who work in my department. There are fewer people working in my department than 10 years ago but I feel that the standards of quality control are much higher now.'

Mark Ryman, Machine Operator

'I've been here for fifteen years and I have seen a few changes in my time. The job used to involve hard physical work and it was dirty too. Now most of the machines are controlled by computers. They work more quickly and accurately than I was ever able to do. I just push the buttons and away it goes. There's not much for me to do now unless something goes wrong. The job is physically less demanding and not so noisy and dirty but in some ways it is less satisfying. Still, I mustn't complain: there are plenty who have lost their jobs through machines taking over.'

questions

1 List all the ways that new technology has affected production at the washing machine factory.
2 How has the company benefited from new technology?
3 Who has lost out through new technology?
4 What is meant by the 'specifications' of a particular machine?
5 What is the purpose of quality control?
6 What is meant by 'everything is produced according to a plan'?

Summary of key words and ideas

- *Bulk reducing* industries tend to be concentrated close to their source of raw materials.
- *Bulk increasing* industries tend to be located close to the market for their product.
- *Industrial inertia* is when the original reasons for a firm's location have disappeared but the firm remains where it is.
- The *division of labour* means dividing work up into small units with workers specialising in particular parts of the production.
- *Productivity* is how much on average each worker produces in a given period of time.
- The *division of labour* normally increases productivity but may result in less job satisfaction.
- The three main methods of organising production are *job*, *batch* and *flow*.
- *Quality control* is checking that the product is being produced according to the standards laid down for it.
- *New technology* can help raise productivity and reduce costs. It may lead to the loss of some workers' jobs and reduce the level of job satisfaction for others. It may also create jobs for other workers and make some tasks less physically demanding and unpleasant.

Suggestions for coursework

1 Location studies: *either*
   a Do a survey of industrial location in your local area trying to find out why firms have decided to locate there, *or*,
   b Compare two different types of area, eg a city centre and a suburb or market town, showing what types of firms are located in each area and indicating why they are there.

2 Division of labour: *either*
   a Show how the division of labour operates in any one firm. Try and interview workers on the production line to see how they feel about the type of work they are doing. Show any ways in which the management is attempting to overcome some of the problems associated with the division of labour, *or*,
   b Set up a classroom experiment where two teams of students have to produce a simple object (eg a paper aeroplane) with a limited amount of capital equipment (scissors, rulers, pencils, etc). One team uses a division of labour and the other works individually. See if the division of labour does result in greater productivity. Write up the results of your experiment as you would in science.

3 The impact of new technology. A study of any one piece of new technology in a firm, eg the introduction of word processors into an office. Try and find out if it has improved productivity, what employees feel about it, whether it has caused any job losses and whether it has involved retraining.

Test questions

1 Oasis is a manufacturer of a range of soft drinks. It is considering setting up a new bottling plant somewhere in the UK. Suggest three things it will need to take into account when deciding where to locate its new factory.

2 Explain one way in which *central government* and one way in which *local government* can influence the location of a firm.

3 Name any manufacturing industry which is normally located close to its market and explain why this is the case.

4 The three methods of organising production are job, batch and flow. Explain what is meant by each of these terms and suggest a product which might be suited to each method.

5 Cars are normally made on an assembly line. Explain what is meant by an assembly line.

6 RK Greens Ltd are a manufacturer of wooden garden furniture. At present each worker on the shop floor makes each individual piece of garden furniture. You are appointed as the new production manager and you propose to reorganise production by introducing a division of labour. This will mean an assembly line with workers each carrying out a small task.
   a What arguments would you put forward for the scheme?
   b Why might some workers resist the introduction of such a scheme?

7 a Describe any piece of new technology.
   b State how the new technology has benefitted the firm.
   c In what ways has the introduction of new technology been, i) an advantage to workers, ii) a disadvantage to workers.

Extension questions

1 A new major airport is to be built in the UK. Which industries is the airport likely to attract which are directly involved with the work of the airport? Which industries not directly connected to the airport are likely to be located in the vicinity? Give reasons for your choice of industries.

2 The division of labour is often said to cause 'worker alienation'.
   a What is meant by the term 'worker alienation'?
   b How can a firm attempt to overcome this problem?

3 'Quality control is about making sure products are of an acceptable standard — this does not mean that they are all perfect.' What do you think of this statement?

Unit 12   The work of the personnel department

aims   At the end of this unit you should understand:

▶   The methods firms use to recruit and select workers.
▶   The need for different types of training.
▶   The different methods of paying workers.
▶   How firms use incentives other than wages to motivate their workforce.
▶   The laws governing the employment of labour.

The personnel department is a very important part of any large company. It is concerned with the recruitment, training, development and welfare of the workforce.

We met Sue Rees, Personnel Manager at Talbot Textiles, in Unit 9. Here is an example of a typically busy day for her.

A day in the life of Sue Rees, Personnel Manager, Talbot Textiles

● *8·15 am* Arrive early to prepare myself for interviews to find a new Sales Manager. Check over applications from the short-listed candidates. Check interview arrangements with secretary.

● *9·00 am* Meeting with Peter Hall, Marketing Manager, to discuss the candidates for the Sales Manager appointment.

● *9·30 am* Start interviews — these go on for the remainder of the morning.

● *12·45 pm* A working lunch with the rest of the interview team to decide upon the appointment.

● *1·45 pm* Back in the office. Meeting with Gill Street, Production Manager, to draft an advertisement to fill a vacancy for a foreman in the weaving shop.

● *2·15 pm* Meeting with union shop stewards to draw up agenda for next Works Council meeting.

● *3·00 pm* Meeting with John West, Training Manager, to discuss YTS training programme.

● *4·00 pm* Read through notes supplied by the Health and Safety Officer on an accident yesterday in the spinning shop. Write memo to Health and Safety Officer suggesting we start disciplinary proceedings.

● *5·00 pm* Meeting with Managing Director to discuss latest pay claim.

exercises   1 List all the different types of work that the Personnel Manager is involved in.
2 List the other departments she needs to involve herself with.

148

Recruitment and selection

COMPUTER NETWORK PRODUCTS

MAJOR ACCOUNTS SALES EXECUTIVE
£30,000 on Target Earnings plus car

YOUNG SALES EXECUTIVES
£25,000 on Target Earnings plus car

VACANCIES

CURTAIN MAKER. Skilled curtain maker (or skilled factory machinist) to work either in workshop or at home. To sew by hand and machine, previously cut pieces of fabric

General Assistant. To help in a local hotel. Silver Service Waiting and general house-keeping duties. Full training given. Some shift work. £40 per week — live in. £55 per week — live

STOCK CONTROL/VDU OPERATOR. Local cosmetics company to feed stock control details into digital computer and to liaise with sales/purchasing and production departments. Experience in VDU operating essential. £4750 to start, rising to £5000 per annum after 3 months trial.

Export Marketing Manager
£12,000   North London

This successful, small company, purchase and re-sell pistachio nuts in the domestic and world market. A recently secured agreement with a German company for the development of sales in the world's export markets, has resulted in them selling this commodity both in the UK and

A knowledge of Plastics &/or Packaging? .....Share in our Success

Part of a major international group, our clients are recognised as a leading force in the plastics/packaging industry and have a reputation for the application of advanced technology to the production process. They are now looking for two experienced people - with exemplary negotiating skills - to join a division which is engaged in the manufacture of injection moulded packaging products. Growing rapidly this particular division has a variety of prestigious UK and overseas customers who in turn supply diverse consumer markets.

It is the job of the Personnel Department to recruit and select workers to fill particular vacancies, from the most junior office assistant up to senior executives. The first step is to advertise the vacancy. Depending upon the job to be filled, this may take the form of local, national or even international advertising.

exercise   All of the above advertisements were taken from either local or national newspapers.

1 Which jobs do you think were advertised locally and which were advertised nationally?
2 How do you think the Personnel Manager in a firm decides whether to advertise locally, nationally or internationally?

Methods of recruitment

JOBCENTRE

International Executive Selection

Advertising in newspapers is only one way of recruiting staff. Firms may also:

- Advertise internally within the firm.
- Advertise on radio and television.
- Notify Job Centres and the Careers Advisory Service.
- Use private recruiting agencies, such as Brook Street Bureau.
- *Headhunt* — some top staff are in such short supply that one firm will recruit direct from another by offering the employee more money and *perks*, such as cars, to join their firm.

Job description and job specification

Before the Personnel Manager advertises a vacancy s/he must decide exactly what the job entails. This is done by writing a *job description* — a definition of the job. This will include details of the responsibilities of the person appointed together with information about hours, holidays, pay and conditions.

The Personnel Manager, in consultation with various departmental managers, also needs to decide in advance what type of person they are looking for. This is known as the *job specification*. This will contain details of the type of qualifications and skills required together with the likely age and experience of the candidate.

Some aspects of the job specification and job description normally appear in the advertisement for the vacancy. Candidates are normally sent more details when they apply for application forms.

exercise

For the following job advertisements:

a List the information contained in each under the headings of Job Description and Job Specification.

b For any two advertisements, say what additional information you would require if you were considering applying for the job.

Applying for a job

The next stage in recruitment is to look at job applications. The following case study looks at it from the applicant's point of view.

Job Vacancy

Job: Office Junior

Employer: Swanson Bookings, High Street, Middleton

Job Description: Swanson Bookings are a travel and theatre booking agency. They require an office junior to assist with basic record keeping, filing and reception duties. 40-hour week. Starting at £45 per week.

Requirements: Minimum age 17. Good GCSE grades in English and Mathematics desirable. Keyboard skills and knowlege of record keeping systems useful.

Applications: By March 10th. Application forms and further details available from the above address.

Ahmed Khan has seen the above job advertisement at his local Careers Office and has decided to apply.

21 The Grove
Sunbury
Kent

20th February 1987

Dear Sir,

Would you please send me application forms and further details for the post of Office Junior at your firm. I enclose a stamped addressed envelope for your reply.

Yours faithfully

A. Khan.

Ahmed's application

The Application Form

SWANSON BOOKINGS
High Street
Middleton
Tel: 0468-382612

APPLICATION FORM

NAME: AHMED KHAN

ADDRESS: 21, The Grove
Sunbury
Kent

TEL NO: 0468 312398

DATE OF BIRTH: 3rd Nov 1970

EDUCATION: Sunbury High
School 1981-present

QUALIFICATIONS: GCSE Maths (D)

(cont) Eng(C) Geog(E)
Bus Studies(C) Int.
Science(E) Craft,Design,
Tech(D)

CURRENT COURSE:
CPVE GCSE (Mature) Maths,
English

INTERESTS: Sport,
reading, photography

ADDITIONAL INFORMATION IN
SUPPORT OF APPLICATION:
I have had work experience
at a Solicitors, Estate
Agency and Travel Agent
and worked part-time at
British Home Stores.

Swanson Bookings
High Street
Middleton
Kent

26th February 1987

Dear Sir,

With reference to the post of Office Junior, I enclose a completed form and include the following additional information in support of my application.

I am at present a 6th form student at Sunbury High School taking the Certificate of Pre-Vocational Education course together with GCSE (Mature) in English and Mathematics.

The CPVE course has allowed me to develop my general education as well as gaining some practical experience of the business world. The course has included three work experience placements and I spent one of these at a local travel agent. I very much enjoyed my time at the travel agency and feel I would like to make this my career.

My CPVE course has also included some keyboarding and word processing and two of my work experience placements offered me the opportunity to try out my skills.

I feel that I would be well suited to the post of Office Junior and ask you to give my application serious consideration.

Yours faithfully

Ahmed Khan.

Letter of Application

Although Swanson Bookings did not ask for them, Ahmed included with his application a copy of his *curriculum vitae* and his *profile* from his school. A curriculum vitae formally sets out the applicant's personal details and experience. The profile is a detailed report which shows the various levels of skill that Ahmed has gained on his CPVE course.

Profile Report

This profile has been issued on the completion of an approved course of study. It has been compiled as a result of regular consultations between scheme tutors and the owner of the profile. The profile has been completed in accordance with the requirements of the Joint Board and has been monitored by the Joint Board. The statements relating to the ten core areas have been selected from the National Bank of Core Competences in accordance with the associated regulations. Evidence for these statements is described on the Summary of Experience which is derived from course work moderated by the Joint Board.

Chairman
Joint Board for Pre-Vocational Education

CURRICULUM VITAE

Name: Ahmed Khan

Address: 21 The Grove,
         Sunbury, Kent

Telephone No. (0468)312398

Marital Status: Single

Date of Birth: 3/11/70

Education: Sunbury High School. 1981-present.

Qualifications: GCSE Maths(D),English(C),Geography(E), Business Studies(C),Integrated Science(E),Craft/ Design/Technology(D)

Current Course: CPVE GCSE(Mature)Maths English.

Employment Experience: Part-time sales assistant British Home Stores. Work experience in Solicitors, Estate Agent and Travel Agent.

Interests: Hockey, Tennis, Travel.

Positions of responsibility: Captain of 1st XI Hockey team. School Prefect

exercise   You are the Personnel Manager at Hollands and Barnett Department Store. You have a vacancy for a part-time sales assistant in the toy department. Wages are £2·50 an hour plus subsidised meals. The hours are Friday 5–8 pm and Saturdays 8·30 am–5·30 pm. Minimum age 17.

a Design an advertisement for the job to go in a local newspaper.
b Prepare an application form for candidates applying for the job.
c Complete an application form and include a letter of application for the job (assume you are 17).

Selection

After the Personnel Manager has received all the applications for a job a *shortlist* of the most appropriate candidates is drawn up. This may be done in consultation with the manager of the department in which the person is going to work. They may well draw up a list of qualities they feel are required for the job.

exercise

1 Draw up a list of qualities you would expect candidates to have for the job at Hollands and Barnett Department Store.
2 Put these in two columns under the headings *Essential Qualities* and *Desirable Qualities*. For example, 'Age 17 +' would be an essential quality while 'previous shop experience' might be a desirable quality.
3 How does Ahmed match up to these qualities?

The interview

The next stage in the selection procedure is to invite the shortlisted candidates for interview. Exactly who does the interviewing will depend upon the size of the company and the importance of the job. In a large company the Personnel Manager may only be involved with appointments at a senior level. Department managers may well be responsible for appointments at a lower level.

Interviews can take many different forms:

- The candidate may be interviewed by one person or by a group of people (known as a panel interview).
- The candidate may be interviewed separately by a number of individuals.
- At higher levels of recruitment candidates are sometimes interviewed as a group in order to discover qualities such as how they get on working with other people, whether they are a group leader and how they react to other viewpoints.
- Candidates may also be subjected to intelligence tests, aptitude tests or asked to write an essay on a particular topic.

Appointment to the job

References

Some firms will ask for references before deciding upon their choice of candidate. They may use references to help them to decide upon their shortlist of candidates. Other firms may only ask for references after they have decided to offer the job to a particular candidate. In this case, the offer of the job will be made 'Subject to suitable references being obtained'.

Firms may also ask for a *testimonial*. This is an open statement from someone who knows the candidate well and normally refers to such qualities as honesty, reliability, etc. The candidate brings this to the interview. This is different from the reference, which is confidential and sent direct to the employer.

The job contract

As soon as a person accepts the offer of a job there is a contract between the employer and the employee even if there is no written contract. Most firms have a written contract which sets out the rights and obligations on both sides, but there is no legal requirement for a firm to have such a contract. The employer is legally obliged, however, to send the employee a written statement of the *terms and conditions* of employment after the worker has been at the firm for 13 weeks. This must include such details as:

- The title of the job.
- The rate of pay.
- Hours of work.
- Holidays.
- Payments during sickness or injury.
- Pension rights.
- Length of notice to be given by the employer or employee to terminate (end) the contract.
- Procedures regarding dismissals.

Some of the employee's rights depend upon the length of time they have been with the firm. (See Unit 13 page 180 for further details)

Contract of Employment

JOB TITLE: Filing clerk
JOB HOLDER: C. Kovaakis
SALARY: £5,200 per annum
HOLIDAY ENTITLEMENT: 21 days per annum in addition to statutory days
HOURS OF WORK: 37 hours per week

Training

Training is a very important part of the Personnel Department's work. In some large firms there is very often a separate training department. Ideally, training should involve the worker before they actually start the job, during the first few weeks of employment and throughout their careers.

The purpose of training

- Train new workers for particular jobs.
- Help to improve the efficiency of existing workers.
- Avoid accidents at work.
- Retrain workers so they can cope with new technology.
- Help workers gain promotion to better jobs within the firm.

case study

Induction training: 'My induction course at Talbot Textiles'

This was my first day at the factory. I can tell you I was pretty nervous when I walked through those factory gates. I wondered what I would be asked to do — I was scared I'd make a fool of myself. I felt better when I was shown to a room with several other new recruits — they all looked as worried as me.

I think we all felt more at ease when the Personnel Manager spoke to us and explained that we wouldn't be thrown onto the production line straight away without any training. He also explained that the purpose of the day was to introduce us to Talbot Textiles. He then told us what his job was in the firm and one or two of us asked some questions about pay and conditions.

We had a very interesting talk by the Production Manager who showed us a short film about what the firm did and how it was organised. This was followed by a talk from the Health and Safety Officer who frightened us by telling us about the sort of accidents that could occur if we didn't stick to the safety code.

After coffee we had a tour round the whole factory. This was useful because it gave us an idea of where we would fit into the organisation. We were also introduced to the people we would be working with.

After lunch we were given talks by a representative from the trade union and by a nurse from the firm's medical room. We finished up with a talk from the secretary of the firm's social club and a final discussion with the Personnel Manager.

Sue, newly appointed machinist

questions

1 What was the purpose of the induction course?
2 How do you think Sue would benefit from the course?
3 If you were joining a new firm, what would you consider to be the most important things to be included in an induction course?

156

Simulated training

After her induction course, Sue spent two days in the department where she was going to work, learning about her job. She was given training on a machine very similar to the one she would be working at but it was not on the production line. The advantage of this was that it could be stopped at any stage if Sue got into difficulty. It also allowed Sue to learn each stage in the process before tackling the whole task.

Job training

After two days, Sue felt confident enough to work on the proper production line. Her supervisor kept a close watch on her and helped her whenever she made an error or was uncertain about what to do.

After a week on the production line, Sue was capable of working unsupervised, but her training did not end there. It was the policy of Talbot Textiles to move workers around in a department so that they understood how to do a range of jobs. Each move meant more training for Sue, first on a simulator and then under supervision on the actual job. Sue enjoyed learning how to do different jobs; it made the work more interesting as well as increasing her skills.

questions

1 What is meant by 'simulated training'?
2 Why do you think firms use simulated training before allowing new recruits to do the actual job?
3 Name another job which would involve simulated training.
4 What is meant by 'on-the-job training'?
5 What advantages are there
  a for Sue,
  b for Talbot Textiles,
  of giving Sue training in a number of different jobs?

Apprenticeship training

An apprenticeship scheme combines practical training at the firm with more theoretical training at a College of Further Education or a Polytechnic. At Talbot Textiles there are a number of different apprenticeship schemes.

Craft and technical apprentices

They mainly joined Talbot Textiles straight from school. They spend a day a week at a local College of Further Education taking BTEC (Business and Technical Education Council) Courses. They are paid by Talbot Textiles whilst they are doing their apprenticeships.

Youth Training Scheme (YTS)

In the last few years, Talbot Textiles has taken on a number of YTS trainees. They are on a two-year course and spend up to three days a week in the factory. The rest of the time they are at the local College of Further Education. They are different from other apprentices in that they are not employees of Talbot Textiles and are paid by the government. Their training is supervised by the College, which acts as *Managing Agent* for the scheme.

Undergraduate apprentices

These apprentices have joined Talbot Textiles after gaining A levels or BTEC National qualifications. They spend some of their time at the factory and the remainder at the Polytechnic where they are studying for HND and Degree qualifications. Most of these apprentices are on what are known as *thick sandwich courses*. This involves blocks of one year at either the Polytechnic or the firm. *Thin sandwich courses* involve shorter blocks at the Polytechnic and at the firm.

Examples of sandwich courses

Thick sandwich
1st year   Firm
2nd year   Polytechnic
3rd year   Firm
4th year   Polytechnic
5th year   Firm
6th year   Polytechnic

DEGREE

Thin sandwich
3 months   Firm
6 months   Polytechnic
3 months   Firm
6 months   Polytechnic
3 months   Firm
6 months   Polytechnic

BTEC HND

Off-the-job training and retraining

Talbot Textiles continues to train and retrain their employees throughout their working lives. They recently sent some of their top managers to learn about a new weaving machine in West Germany with a view to installing it at Talbot Textiles. If they decide to buy the new machine, it will involve sending some of the workforce on training courses in West Germany so that they are able to use the equipment as soon as it is installed.

The government and training

TRAINING FOR SKILLS

From April 1986, YTS will take a giant step forward:

- a two year training programme for 16 year olds with at least 20 weeks off-the-job training over two years;
- a one year programme for 17 year olds with at least seven weeks off-the-job training;

- the opportunity for all young people to obtain recognised vocational qualifications which indicate competence in the workplace;
- a Training Agreement for all who take part spelling out what is involved in the training programme;
- nationally agreed standards of training.

All political parties recognise the importance of training and retraining. A skilled workforce helps to make British industry more efficient and competitive.

In 1973 the government set up the Manpower Services Commission (MSC) to look after employment and training. The MSC (now the Training Agency) is responsible for the Youth Training Scheme, which involves a large number of school and college leavers.

The Training Agency (TA) is also responsible for a number of Training Centres in Britain, particularly in areas of high unemployment. Here, workers can learn new skills or retrain for new jobs. The Job Training Scheme (which replaces the Training Opportunities Scheme) offers retraining courses for both employed and unemployed workers and pays a grant during the course.

The TA also administers the Industrial Training Boards which were set up in 1964. These were established for 24 different types of industry and their task is to co-ordinate training and help financially in sponsoring different programmes.

A recent development has been the Technical and Vocational Education Initiative (TVEI) where the TA has helped to fund certain courses in schools and colleges with a view to improving job skills.

Paying the workers

Contract Hire Manager

£22-25,000 + Car

JOBCENTRE

Exceptional Role in Training

£25,000 + Car + Benefits

VACANCIES

DISPLAY ASSISTANT. To work in a town centre department store arranging window displays, internal banners, ticketing, etc. You should preferably have had some experience or have an artistic flair. Wage: £2.17 per hour + staff discount. Hours: 8.50am-5.35pm Mon-Fri. **Ref 7217.**

CASUAL FARM LABOURER required, £2 per hour. Must be reli-

COOK SUPERVISOR

26¼ hours per week, term time only. Wage £68.83 inclusive of plus rate. Application forms available from and returnable to the

Wages and salaries

Staff workers are paid an annual *salary*. This is divided into twelve equal parts and normally paid directly into the employee's bank account each month by a credit transfer. The amount paid each month does not usually vary a great deal because staff workers do not tend to receive overtime or piece-rate payments (see below).

Wages are paid each week. *Manual workers* are still often paid wages in *cash*. The amount paid each week may vary considerably, depending upon overtime and bonus payments.

Methods of payment

- There are two basic methods of paying workers:
  1 By time, known as *time rate*.
  2 By what the worker produces, known as *piece rate*.
  Some firms combine both these methods. They pay so much for a 40-hour week and a *bonus* if the worker produces more than a certain target level of production. A special form of piece-rate payment is known as *commission*. This is often applied to salesmen who get paid according to what they sell in the form of a percentage of the value of the sales.
- *Overtime* payment is for hours worked over and above the basic week. This is normally paid at a higher rate than the basic wage, eg a worker gets paid £6 per hour and 'time and a half' for overtime. This means that each hour of overtime is paid at £9 an hour.

Note Staff workers are not normally paid overtime but some firms have a system of *flexitime*. An example of such a system would be to require staff to work a minimum 40-hour week and allow them to start and finish work at any time provided that they were at the firm between the 'core' hours of 10 am–4 pm. If staff work more than 40 hours in a week they are allowed time off: if they have 8 hours *credit* they are allowed a *flexiday* holiday.

160

exercises

1 For each of the following workers say which methods of payment you feel would be most appropriate giving reasons for your choice. Set out your answer as shown.

Methods: wage/salary, time rate/piece rate, commission, overtime, bonus

Workers: Supermarket checkout operator, double-glazing salesperson, knitwear outworker (this is someone working for a firm from home), company accountant, delivery driver, assembly-line worker in electronics factory

Supermarket checkout operator. Wage – Time Rate – Overtime.
Reasons: Fixed hours/need longer hours for late night opening and Christmas period/ difficult to apply piece rate methods.

2 Try to find examples of jobs from advertisements in local and national newspapers which illustrate the following methods of payment: salary, wage, time rate, piece rate, commission, bonus.

3 Put the following statements under the headings of *time rate* and *piece rate* depending upon which one you feel they refer to:
— Difficult to apply to jobs where each person's output is difficult to measure.
— Can be applied to almost any job.
— More suited to production of a good than a service.
— Gives an incentive to workers to produce as much as they can.
— Workers may waste time because they get paid whether they produce or not.
— May lead to poor workmanship and the need for a great deal of quality control because workers are tempted to work too quickly.

4 Josh gets paid £5 an hour as a machine operator. His basic week is 40 hours and he gets time and a half for any work done on top of this.
   a How much does he get paid in a normal week?
   b How much would he get paid if he worked 45 hours in a week?
   c How many hours overtime did he work if he got paid £230 last week?

5 You are a sales-person for a firm making birthday and Christmas cards. You currently get paid a regular salary but the firm wants to alter this and pay you mainly on commission. Explain whether you would be for or against this change.

The pay slip

Pay Slip   J.C. SWEETMAN LTD

NAME	PAY No.	MONTH	DEPT	N.I. NUMBER
F.R. JONES	8031670	SEPT 1987	038	YP31-498-670

PAY TO DATE	TAX TO DATE	SUPPN. TO DATE	N.I. TO DATE	TAX CODE
4660.11	905.80	335.71	224.31	156L

GROSS PAY	OVERTIME etc	GROSS PAY AFTER ADJUSTMENT	SUPN.	INCOME TAX	N.I.
772		77.2	50.00	180.00	25.00

NET PAY

exercise

1 Calculate F. R. Jones net pay for September 1987.
2 What other information might be included on the pay slip?
3 What percentage of income does F. R. Jones lose in deductions?
4 What is the purpose of the deductions? How does the Government make use of the money it takes from the pay packet?

Notes

- NI = National Insurance Contributions   This is money paid to the Government which is used to finance such things as sickness and injury benefits.
- SUPN = Superannuation   This is money used by the government to help pay for pensions.
- Tax Code   This shows how much a person is allowed before they are taxed. A married man, for example, gets a higher allowance than a single person. Every worker is notified of their tax code each year by the Inland Revenue.
- Gross Pay is pay before deductions for National Insurance, Superannuation and Tax are made.
- Net Pay is what the worker actually receives after deductions are made.
- PAYE (Pay As You Earn)   Most employees pay tax each month to the Inland Revenue. It is deducted automatically from their wages and is shown on the pay slip.

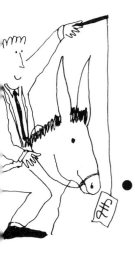

Motivating the worker

It is part of the Personnel Department's job to try to make sure that the workforce is well motivated and that each worker is keen to do their best. A well motivated workforce helps to raise productivity and reduce the number of days' work lost through absenteeism and strikes.

How do we increase motivation?

In order to find ways of increasing motivation we need to look at the reasons why people work — what satisfactions do they get from their work?

- Probably the most important reason for people working is the pay they receive at the end of the week or month which can then be used for buying goods and services.

Pay is not the only satisfaction people get from work.

- Workers may get satisfaction from making something well or achieving an objective, eg a potter may get satisfaction from making a beautiful vase, a manager may get satisfaction from increasing the sales in his department.
- Workers may gain status by being in positions of authority and leadership.
- Workers may enjoy the social side of work — meeting other people in 'formal' groups (departments, sections etc), or in 'informal' groups (eg groups of friends meeting in the canteen).

Rewarding workers: pay and perks

The chance to earn higher pay clearly helps to motivate workers. This may be achieved through promoting members of the workforce to higher paid positions or by offering various bonus schemes. For example, a firm may give a bonus to workers in a particular department for increasing productivity (output per worker) by a certain amount.

Firms may also give non-monetary rewards, such as cars, houses, holidays, expense accounts, first-class travel, and discounts on the firm's products. These are sometimes called the *perks* of the job.

Other ways of improving motivation

- Training schemes which help workers to gain promotion or do more skilled work.
- Making the work more interesting by giving workers larger tasks to do, perhaps working in a group.
- Giving workers more responsibility.
- Involving workers in making decisions which affect their lives.
- *Profit sharing* If workers know that they are going to get a share of the profits, it will be an incentive for them to try and help the firm gain larger profits. Some firms do this by making their workers shareholders in the company and paying them partially in extra shares (a worker cooperative would be an extreme form of this).

- *Report writing* Some firms have a system of report writing which identifies each worker's strengths and weaknesses. This is then discussed with the worker in an open way. This makes sure that each manager or supervisor takes an interest in the progress of the workers he is responsible for.
- *Social facilities* Many firms have found that offering good social facilities, such as sports clubs and subsidised canteens, helps to motivate the workforce.
- Giving workers a feeling of 'belonging'. Large Japanese firms and some American companies place a great deal of emphasis upon loyalty to the organisation. They help to gain loyalty by looking after both the financial and non-financial needs of their workforce and families.
- *Suggestion boxes*

Workers are encouraged to suggest ways of improving production and are awarded bonuses if their ideas are successful.

exercise

You are Personnel Manager at a large manufacturing firm. Suggest ways of increasing the motivation of the following workers:

a Production-line workers with little possibility of promotion.
b A middle manager who has been doing the same job for 10 years.
c A new recruit in the Finance Department.
d A salesperson

Summary of key words and ideas

- The *Personnel Department* is concerned with the recruiting, training, promotion and welfare of the workforce.
- *job description* is a definition of what the job involves.
- *job specification* is a statement of the qualities a firm is looking for to fill a vacancy.
- *Applications* for jobs may involve the completion of forms, a letter of application and a curriculum vitae (details of a person's experience, under headings).
- Taking up a post involves a *contract* which places certain legal obligations on both the firm and the person being employed.
- *Training* may involve: *induction* (an introduction to the firm), *simulated training* (learning on a simplified version of the real job), *on-the-job training* (learning whilst actually doing the job), *off-the-job training* (training courses away from the firm), *apprenticeships* (a combination of work and study at an educational institution).
- *Sandwich courses* involve blocks of work alternating with blocks of time in education.
- The *Training Agency* (previously the MSC) is responsible for government training and retraining schemes.
- *Time rate* is being paid according to the number of hours, weeks or months worked.
- *Piece rate* is being paid according to how much is produced.
- *Commission* is earnings in the form of a percentage of the sales a person makes.

Suggestions for coursework

1 Imagine that you are the Personnel Manager in a firm.
   a Decide on a job vacancy.
   b Write a job description and a job specification.
   c Prepare an advertisement to go in a local newspaper.
   d Make a list, in order of importance, of the qualities you will be looking for in a candidate for the job.
   e Draw up an application form for the job.
2 For any one firm, investigate the types of training that the firm uses. Try and obtain interviews with workers who have undergone different forms of training to find out its nature and how they felt they had benefited from it.
3 *Either*, do a survey of local Youth Training Schemes finding out: how they operate,
   what trainees like and dislike about them,
   the number of trainees who get taken on in full time employment, etc.
   Or,
   Do a survey of job vacancies in the local area, using newspapers, Job Centres, and the Careers Advisory Service. Find out:

the type of employment being offered,
the wages and salaries being paid,
what type of person is required.
Try to draw some general conclusions about job vacancies in your
local area.

Test questions

JOB CENTRE	
POST	Trainee Accounts Clerk
FIRM	S W Brindley Engineering Ltd
DISTRICT	South Moulton
SALARY	Starting at £3800 (rising to £4500 on completion of training). Plus fringe benefits and profit sharing.
HOURS	40 hour week. Monday - Friday. Flexitime working.
TRAINING	Day and block release available plus on the job training.
REQUIREMENTS	Minimum age 18, good general education including high grade GCSE Maths and English. A Level preferred.
APPLICATIONS	By letter of application to Personnel Manager.
(S W Brindley is an Equal Opportunities Employer)	

1 What is a job centre?
2 Describe two other ways in which SW Brindley could try to recruit labour.
3 Name two 'fringe benefits' the firm might offer.
4 What is meant by 'profit sharing'? What is its purpose?
5 How would 'flexitime' operate if the 'core hours' were 10 am–4 pm?
6 What is meant by,
   a day release,
   b block release,
   c on-the-job training?
7 Describe two other types of training the firm might use.
8 List all the information contained in the advertisement under the headings of Job Description and Job Specification.
9 What does 'equal opportunities employer' mean?
10 Imagine you are 18 with the qualifications required for the post. Write a letter of application to SW Brindley.

Extension questions

1 Compare the likely job satisfaction of a nurse with that of a production line worker in an electronics factory.
2 Describe two ways, apart from pay, of increasing worker motivation.
3 What are the advantages and disadvantages of using,
   a time rate,
   b piece rate,
   as methods of paying workers?

Unit 13　Industrial relations

aims　At the end of this unit you should understand:

▶　The reasons for the existence of trade union and employer associations.
▶　The different types of trade unions and professional associations.
▶　How trade unions are organised.
▶　How collective bargaining is carried out.
▶　The causes of conflict between workers and employers.
▶　The legal rights of workers and employers.

case study — Why join a union?

Scene:	Josie has recently joined the printing department of Talbot Textiles. She is having a coffee in the canteen with Marie. Marie has worked at Talbot Textiles for ten years.
Marie:	Are you coming to the union meeting at lunchtime then?
Josie:	No, I'm not a member. I can't be bothered with all that sort of thing.
Marie:	You ought to join.
Josie:	What for? They never do anything, do they? Besides, I'm quite happy, I don't want to go around stirring up trouble!
Marie:	The union has done a lot here to improve things. And there's been just the one strike since I've been here — and that only lasted for a week.
Josie:	What are all these things the union's supposed to do then?
Marie:	Well, they negotiate our pay each year. I know the wages are nothing to write home about, but they would be a lot worse if we didn't join together to present our case. We'd just have to accept what the firm offered us if there was no union. They know we'd take action if we didn't get something like a reasonable deal. But pay isn't the only thing the union's concerned about. Last year they helped us get two days' extra holiday. They've improved conditions too. They helped persuade the management to get that new extractor fan installed in our area. And this new canteen was a result of a meeting between the union and the management — we do work together, you know. We're not always at each others' throats.
Josie:	Well, I'm still not sure. I don't know whether I can afford it.
Marie:	That's ridiculous. Look at the benefits you get. How would you pay legal fees if you were injured and had to take them to court to get compensation? Who would fight your case if they tried to dismiss you or make you redundant? I suppose you'd just accept it!

exercises

1 Make a list of all the reasons mentioned in the case study for being a union member.

2 'I know the wages are nothing to write home about, but they would be a lot worse if we didn't join together to present our case.' Marie is referring here to what is known as *collective bargaining*. Explain in your own words what collective bargaining involves and how it benefits the worker.

More functions of trade unions

Apart from the things mentioned in the case study, trade unions also:

- Support training and education.
- Help finance certain Members of Parliament.
- Act as a *pressure group* by trying to influence the Government.
- Help negotiate contracts and conditions of employment.
- Some unions offer insurance cover to their members and negotiate discounts on certain goods and services. They may also offer cheap leisure and holiday facilities for their members as well as social benefits for a worker's family in the event of premature death.

Types of unions

There are about 12 million trade union members in the UK. This is just over half of the working population. About one third of the members are women. Just under two thirds of union members are manual workers. The largest union is the Transport and General Workers Union with over 2 million members. Some unions, such as the Scottish Union of Power Loom Overlookers, have fewer than 250 members. Unions can be grouped into different types:

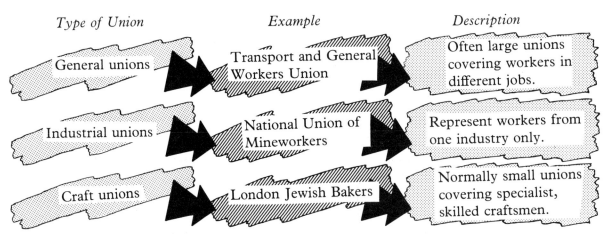

Type of Union	Example	Description
General unions	Transport and General Workers Union	Often large unions covering workers in different jobs.
Industrial unions	National Union of Mineworkers	Represent workers from one industry only.
Craft unions	London Jewish Bakers	Normally small unions covering specialist, skilled craftsmen.

In addition to these types, some unions are called *white collar unions*. These are unions for non-manual workers, often in the service sector. The National Union of Bank Employees is an example of a white collar union but it could also be classified as an industrial union as it represents workers from one industry.

Professional and employer associations

Some professions such as solicitors, surveyors and accountants have *associations* rather than unions to look after their interests. These associations often have strict entry requirements which only allow membership to those who have qualified to a particular standard in the profession. Examples of such associations include the Institute of Chartered Accountants, The Law Society and the British Medical Association.

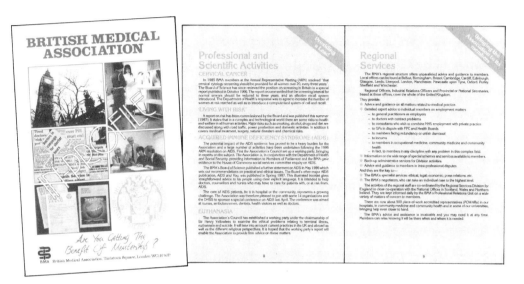

Employers also have their own organisations. Such organisations as The National Federation of Building Trades Employers look after their member firms by negotiating with unions and trying to influence the Government on matters which are of concern to them. Many employers are members of the Confederation of British Industry (CBI). This organisation acts on behalf of its members by carrying out research, publishing surveys and trying to influence Government economic thinking.

exercises

a Match the pairs in the following columns:

Example	*Type of Union/Association*
Amalgamated Society of Carpenters and Joiners	General Union
National Union of Railwaymen	Professional Association
General and Municipal Workers Union	Employer Association
Chemical Industries Association	Craft Union

b 'General Unions are often very large but are not as powerful as smaller Industrial Unions or Craft Unions'.
Why do you think this may be the case?

How trade unions are organised

The Trades Union Congress (TUC)

Most, but not all, unions are members of the TUC. The TUC does not have the power to tell individual unions how to run their affairs, although it can advise them to take a particular course of action. The TUC, through its General Council, represents the views of its members to the Government and attempts to influence policy. The TUC also carries out research into various aspects of the trade union movement and publishes a wide range of policy documents. The TUC will, on occasions, help to settle industrial disputes — particularly disputes between unions. The TUC meets once a year for its conference to debate various motions and elect members to the General Council. The Council attempts to put the decisions made at the conference into action during the rest of the year.

People in the union

Not all unions are organised in the way shown n the diagram on the previous page. Different types of unions also have different names for their officials. White collar unions have *representatives* rather than shop stewards. In the print unions, the local branch is called a *chapel* and the shop stewards are called *fathers of the chapel*.

Shop stewards are the elected representatives of the members in the workplace. Large firms will have several shop stewards who meet together with the *convener* of the shop stewards — a type of chairman. Shop stewards are full-time employees of the firm and are not paid for their work by the union.

Depending upon the size of the union, there will be full-time, paid employees of the union who carry out the union's work at local, branch and national level. These officials may be elected by the members or appointed by the union.

Profile: Sam Collins, Shop Steward, Talbot Textiles

'I've been at Talbot Textiles for 6 years now. I joined straight from school and spent four years in the weaving shop before moving to finishing. The people I worked with in weaving persuaded me to join the union and I've got more and more involved. I've always been prepared to put my views forward and I guess that's how I got elected as a shop steward last year.

My job is to represent the views of the 30 members in my part of the factory. I also attend meetings with the convener of the shop stewards. He discusses what's been happening at branch and national level in the union. The convener also meets with the Personnel Manager at the Works Council meetings. I take all this information back to our members on the shop floor at our regular meetings.

The union has given me some training in industrial relations and this has already been useful. Just last week I helped sort out a problem to do with sick pay for one of our members with the Personnel Manager. Last month there was a problem with a change of shift working hours. This could have led to a real dispute if I hadn't got the matter settled through our Works Council.

I'm the first person the members in our section turn to if there's a problem. I try and get the matter settled before it becomes a big issue. We want to avoid industrial action if possible — that doesn't do anyone any good.'

Profile: June Williams, full-time union official

'I spent the first 10 years of my working life on the production line at a biscuit factory. There was no union when I started and conditions were terrible. Some of us joined the Transport and General Workers Union to see if we could do anything to improve matters. I suppose they elected me as their shop steward because I was prepared to say what I thought to the management.

I got really involved in the union when we had a strike for higher pay. Sometime after this I was asked if I was interested in working for the union full-time. I jumped at the opportunity and the union paid for me to go to college and attend their training course.

I find the work very interesting. My job is to get to know all I can about the local firms our members are employed in. This helps me to assist the shop stewards in obtaining the best deal for their members. I also have to know about union policy so that I can inform branch members about what's going on. I meet regularly with the conveners of the shop stewards and attend as many meetings of our members as possible. It's my job to recommend to the union that a strike becomes 'official'. I am also responsible for organising elections and ballots in our area and making sure that they are carried out according to the requirements laid down by the union.'

exercises   **a** Describe a day in the life of either a shop steward or a full-time union official to show as many of their functions as possible.

b List the functions of the person you did *not* choose in (a).

174

Industrial disputes

Some facts

- The UK does not have a bad strike record compared with other countries.
- 90% of industrial disputes are settled without the need for strike action.
- Many more days of work are lost through accidents, sickness and absenteeism (unexplained absences) than through strikes.
- 90% of strikes are *unofficial* — they do not have the official approval of the union.

---

case study

Bakery Workers Threaten Strike Action

Workers at the Freshbake factory were last night threatening strike action if the management did not substantially improve their latest pay offer. Negotiations between the employers side and the union finally broke down after four hours of discussions. Convener of shop stewards, Bob Morris, said after the meeting, 'The management just can't see sense. Their offer is totally unreasonable. The bakery made very substantial profits last year and the workers want a share of them. We're not asking for a fortune — just comparability with other workers in the industry. The pay at Freshbake has fallen well behind what other bakery workers are getting throughout the country.'

Managing Director, Pam Brown, commented, 'The offer is a very reasonable one. It gives all workers at least an 8% rise — that's a real increase of 5% when you take account of the rate of inflation.

Freshbake can't afford to pay any more than this — we have our shareholders to think of too.'

---

questions

a What is the cause of the dispute?

b What does *comparability* mean?

c What is the management's case?

d What does *a real increase of 5%* mean?

e What was the rate of inflation?

f Explain what is meant by 'we have our shareholders to think of too'.

Strike to go on

The strike at Freshbake, now in its second week, looks like continuing after workers rejected an improved pay offer from the management. A round-the-clock picket line has been maintained outside the factory and delivery drivers have refused to cross it. 'Most workers, union and non-union, have not crossed the picket line and production is at a standstill' said Bob Morris, convener. Management agreed that the strike was proving to be very costly in terms of lost output. 'We are losing something like £10 000 a day at the moment,' said Managing Director, Pam Brown. 'We needed to reduce the workforce this year and we were hoping to do it by voluntary redundancies and natural wastage, but this strike will mean some compulsory redundancies now.'

Terms

Picketing

This is when union members stand outside the workplace and try to persuade fellow workers not to go to work by handing out leaflets and explaining the reasons for the dispute. 'Crossing the picket line' means entering the factory when it is being picketed.

The law and picketing

Picketing has been a sensitive area in industrial relations during the past few years. Only peaceful picketing is allowed and fellow workers must not be intimidated by the picket line. *Secondary picketing* is when pickets come from workplaces not directly involved in the dispute; this is now illegal.

Redundancy

This is when workers lose their jobs because the firm needs less labour. This is different from being sacked or dismissed because of poor timekeeping, failure to do the job, etc. Workers who are made redundant are entitled to compensation — the amount depends upon their current earnings and how long they have been with the firm. Voluntary redundancies are when workers accept redundancy without it being made compulsory — early retirement is an example of this.

Natural wastage

There will normally be a turnover of staff during the year with workers retiring, leaving for other jobs or taking maternity leave. A firm can reduce its labour force if these workers are not replaced by others. This is referred to as natural wastage.

exercise Before reading on in the case study, try and think of a solution to the dispute at Freshbake. The management have now offered 9% and cannot afford any more without something in return. The unions have reduced their claim from 12% to 11% and are determined to continue with the strike.

How the Freshbake dispute was settled

The strike went on for a further two weeks before both sides agreed to refer the matter to ACAS. This is the Government's Advisory, Conciliation and Arbitration Service. A *conciliator* was appointed to help settle the dispute. A conciliator is an impartial person whose job is to bring the two sides in a dispute together to try to find grounds for a settlement.

(*Note*   In some disputes the matter is referred to *arbitration*. The arbitrator, or panel of arbitrators, looks into the dispute and makes a recommendation as to how it can be settled. Both sides may agree to accept the decision before the report is made.)

After more discussions, the management at Freshbake agreed to increase their offer to 10.5%. In return, the union agreed to some voluntary redundancies, a more flexible shift system and a productivity deal. The deal was accepted by the members of the union and there was a rapid return to work.

questions

a Suggest how the strike at Freshbake could have been avoided.
b How was Freshbake eventually able to pay more than a 9% increase?
c What is a productivity deal?
d Describe how a shift system operates over 24 hours.
e How might a flexible shift system work?

A role play

The situation   Aero-Devices Ltd. is a medium-sized 'high-tech' electronics firm making components for the aircraft industry. The firm has recently won a large order which it needs to meet urgently. In order to do this it wants to introduce a new system of flexible working.

The workers   You are used to working a regular 40-hour week and are opposed to the plan for a new system of working. This will involve working early and late shifts as well as some weekend work.

The managers   You must fulfil the order on time otherwise a large financial penalty will be imposed on you. The new shift system will help increase productivity which is vital if the deadline is to be met. You are prepared to offer normal overtime rates for weekend working but are keen to keep other wage costs as low as possible.

The independent arbitrator   Your presence has been agreed to by both parties involved in the dispute. You must listen to both sides of the argument and then put forward a solution to the dispute.

The role play starts with the management announcing that the firm has won the new order and its plans for flexible working.

case study

A demarcation dispute

There are two main unions at Smith Brothers, a firm making wooden garden furniture. The Craft Union represents the skilled carpenters and joiners. The General Union represents less skilled manual workers. The skilled workers are paid more highly than the other workers.

Smith Brothers have recently been taken over by another firm. The new management have decided to revolutionize production methods by introducing new machinery which will enable the furniture to be mass produced on a flow line. The new methods involve less skill and the management proposes to abolish the distinction between craft and general workers. It is intended to pay all workers at the craft rate as they will all be doing similar jobs.

The proposal has provoked a hostile reaction from the craft workers. They have already banned all overtime working and are considering taking further action in the form of a *go slow* or a *work to rule*.

The Craft Union objects to the loss of pay *differentials* and fears that their members may lose jobs in the future to the general workers. They consider that *custom and practice* means that certain jobs are only done by their members.

The General Union is equally determined that their members will receive the same pay as the craft workers for doing identical work.

Terms

Demarcation dispute

A dispute between two unions as to who does what work. One function of a union is to protect members' jobs and this includes the taking over of jobs by members from another union.

Go slow

Deliberately working at a slower pace. It is difficult for the management to do anything about this if workers are not being paid piece rate.

Work to rule

Working completely according to the rule book. This might involve carrying out long winded safety checks, not working in certain conditions, etc. This has the effect of slowing down production and there is again very little the management can do about it.

Differential

The difference in pay between one group of workers and another. Skilled workers may object to an 'erosion of differentials' because they expect to be paid more than less skilled workers.

Custom and practice

This is when something has been done in a particular way for a long period of time. Even though this is not written down anywhere it may be accepted as law in certain cases.

exercises

a As a representative of the Craft Union, make a case out to an arbitrator as to why you oppose the management scheme.

b Make a case out to an arbitrator as a representative of the General Union.

c What decision would you make as the arbitrator in the dispute?

More terms

Lock out

This is action taken by an employer to prevent workers from entering the workplace. Employers may do this in a dispute if they feel that workers will severely disrupt production in some way.

Closed shop

Where workers have to be a member of a particular union to work at a firm. At present it looks likely that the closed shop will not be legally enforcable as it is regarded as a 'restrictive practice'.

Works council

A committee made up of representatives from the workforce, and from management, which meets regularly to discuss problems and to make suggestions as to how they might be best dealt with. This is a form of *industrial democracy* — allowing workers to have a say in the running of the firm.

Grievance procedure

An agreement made between the unions and the employer as to the steps to be taken in the case of industrial problems and disputes. This normally involves an agreement not to take industrial action before the matter is referred to a particular body.

The legal rights of individuals at work

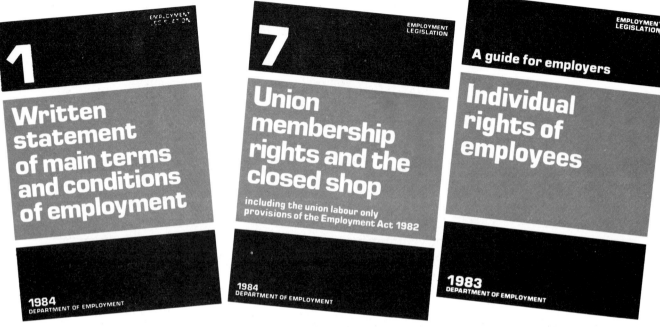

- As soon as a person accepts the offer of a job, there is a contract between the employer and the employee even though there may be nothing in writing.
- After 13 weeks the employee is entitled to a written statement of the *terms and conditions of employment* (see Unit 12).
- After one month's employment, the employee, if s/he wants to leave, must give at least one week's notice that they intend leaving. This may be longer if it is stated in the job contract.
- The length of notice an employer must give to an employee depends upon the length of time a person has been working at a firm. After one month, they are entitled to a minimum of one week's notice; after two years, they must be given two weeks' notice; after three years, three weeks, and so on, up to twelve weeks for twelve or more years service. The contract may specify longer periods of notice which an employee is legally entitled to.
- An employee is legally entitled to a written explanation if they are dismissed after having worked at a firm for six months or more.
- Employees who have been working for a firm for a minimum of two years can appeal to an *industrial tribunal* if they feel that they have been unfairly dismissed. (The two-year rule does not apply in the case of dismissals on grounds of sex, ethnic group, or trade union membership — see below). Tribunals are set up under the guidance of ACAS and consist of a legal expert and one representative from the employer's side and one from the employee's side. The employee will be reinstated (given their job back) or offered compensation if it is found that they have been unfairly dismissed.

- Employees who are made redundant by a firm and who have worked for them for two years or more, are entitled to a lump sum redundancy payment. The amount of this depends upon the length of time a person has been with a firm and their earnings at the time of being made redundant.

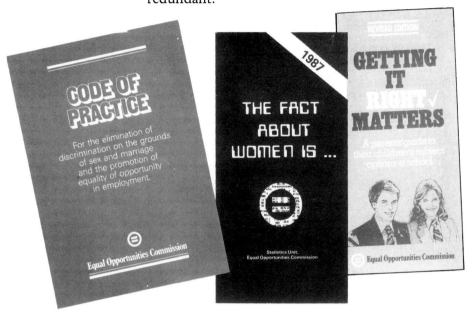

- *Equal Opportunities* Workers are not allowed to be discriminated against on grounds of ethnic group or sex. This applies to recruitment, pay and promotion. A person who feels that they have been discriminated against can appeal to the Equal Opportunities Commission or the Commission for Racial Equality.
- Women who have been with a firm in full-time employment for two years or more are entitled to maternity pay for six weeks during the eleven weeks before the baby is due. Provided that they have been working with the firm for two years, women are entitled to their job back up to 29 weeks after the baby is born.

Equal pay success for canteen girls

Women canteen workers at R.K. Factors have been awarded substantial pay increases following an Equal Opportunities Commission ruling. The women claimed parity of pay with male workers on the factory floor. The E.O.C. agreed that the work of the canteen staff was equal to production line workers. R.K. Factors had claimed that the work of the canteen workers was less skilled than the assembly workers . . .

---

questions

1 Is working in a canteen as skilled as assembly-line work?
2 Should equal work always be rewarded by equal pay?

Summary of key words and ideas

- *Collective bargaining* When a union negotiates with an employer on behalf of a group of workers rather than each worker negotiating individually.
- *Unions* look after their members' interests in terms of pay, conditions, and job protection. They also assist in training and education and attempt to influence Government policy.
- *Shop stewards* represent the members at factory level. They are employees of the firm and are not paid by the union for their work.
- *Full-time union officials* are paid by the union for their work in organising union matters at branch and national level.
- *Unofficial strikes* are those strikes which have not received official backing from the union. 90% of strikes are unofficial.
- *Pay comparability* is receiving similar pay for similar jobs.
- *Real wage* is the amount a person receives after inflation is taken into account. It is what the wage is worth in terms of the goods and services it will buy.
- Workers and shareholders both make demands on the profits of a company. The proportion each group obtains depends upon the outcome of pay bargaining each year.
- The *Advisory, Conciliation and Arbitration Service* is a Government agency set up to help settle industrial disputes. It does not have the power to enforce a settlement in a dispute but offers advice and appoints neutral conciliators and arbitrators.
- A *demarcation dispute* is a dispute between unions over who does what job.

Suggestions for coursework

a Follow an industrial dispute through from start to finish using newspapers, television and radio. Show how the dispute came about, how it developed and how it was settled.

b Find out how industrial relations operate in one large firm. Try and obtain interviews with a shop steward and a personnel manager to find out their roles and how they operate during disputes. How do the firm and the unions attempt to settle disputes? What are the main causes of industrial disputes in the firm?

c Act out the role play on page 177. Write a detailed account of the background to the dispute, the events which take place, and how it is settled.

Test questions

1 As a shop steward, make out a list of reasons why a new recruit to your firm should join the union.
2 Explain the difference between,
   a a general union,
   b a craft union,
   c an industrial union.
   Give an example of each type.
3 What is the purpose of the Confederation of British Industry (CBI)?
4 What is the purpose of the TUC?
5 Briefly explain the function of each of the following:
   a shop steward,
   b convener of shop stewards,
   c full-time union official,
   d General Secretary of a union.
6 Name four causes of industrial disputes.
7 What is meant by an unofficial strike?
8 Describe how ACAS might help to settle a dispute.
9 Describe three types of industrial action a union may take, apart from strikes.

Extension questions

1 A decline in orders for the car components firm of CT Lewis means that 50 fewer workers are needed. The union accepts the need for some redundancies but has put forward four suggestions as to how the firm could avoid making all of them compulsory.
   a Explain the difference between redundancy and sacking.
   b What four suggestions do you think the union might put forward?
2 Explain why unions will take account of the rate of inflation when they submit their wage claims.
3 'Unions increase wages and make it more difficult for workers to get jobs'.
   'Without unions, wages would be lower and more workers would lose their jobs'.
   Explain both these statements.
4 'Most of the work of unions is not concerned with pay disputes'.
   Explain what areas unions are engaged in apart from wage negotiations.

Unit 14   Marketing and selling in a large firm

aims   At the end of this unit you should understand:

► The stages in the life cycle of a product.
► How large firms carry out market research.
► Advertising and sales promotion methods used by large firms.
► How the consumer is protected.
► The different methods of transport available and their relative merits.

Product life cycle

New products pass through a series of stages, and this is called their *life cycle*. This is particularly true of *branded products*. A brand is the *trade name* for a particular good eg (baked beans) Heinz, Crosse and Blackwell, HP, Tesco.

---

case study   ### Life cycle of the Scout chocolate bar

Stage 1   Research and development

Features   Market research, product design and development. Advertising and sales tests in selected areas.

Profits   No sales, high fixed costs of research and development. Loss making.

Stage 2   Introduction

Features   The launch of the product on the national market. Heavy advertising and sales promotion. Introductory special offers to tempt public into trying the product.

Profits   High initial sales revenue because of *novelty* of new product and *head start* on competitors. But high fixed costs and special offers mean that an overall loss is being made.

Stage 3   Growth

Features   Product now being established in the market. Advertising and promotion less intense than in introductory stage, but remains important.

Profits   More profit being made on each unit but total costs still not covered.

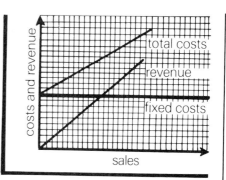

Stage 4   Maturity (saturation)

Features   Product well established in market. Competitive advertising to keep product in the mind of the public. Sales promotions to maintain market position for as long as possible.

Profits   Period of maximum sales. Total costs now being covered. Overall profit being made.

Stage 5   Decline

Features   Introduction of rival brands and competitive advertising. Patent may expire allowing more competition. Changes in style and taste. Loss of market share. Advertising and sales promotions fail to regain share.

Profits   Declining profits but still adding to total profits on the brand.

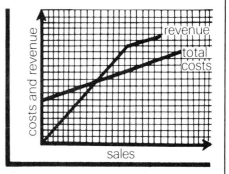

Stage 6   Obsolescence

Features   Decision made to stop production of brand. Stocks sold off at reduced rate. Little or no advertising expenditure.

Profits   Products sold at reduced profit or cost to avoid unsold stock and losses. Overall substantial profit made. Some profits invested in developing new line.

1 Choose any product and make a list of at least five brand names.
2 How do the manufacturers of the product you have chosen try and make their brand seem different from another firm's brand?
3 Why did it take until Stage 4 of the product life cycle before an overall profit on the Scout Bar was made?
4 'Win a holiday of a lifetime' was the method of sales promotion chosen by the manufacturers of Scout Bar. Name three other methods of sales promotion that firms use.
5 Name two brands of different products which are now obsolete.

More about market research

Large firms spend a great deal of time and money on market research in order to get their product design correct. Firms may either carry out the research themselves or employ a market research agency to do the work for them. A new product line will involve a firm in considerable expenditure on new machinery, marketing and advertising — so it must make sure that its product will sell enough to recover its costs and make a profit.

case study

The launch of Yorkie Bar

Background

The market for chocolate in the UK is a very competitive one and is dominated by Cadbury-Schweppes and Rowntree-Mackintosh. During the 1970s, sales of bars of chocolate were declining. This was partly due to a rapid rise in the price of cocoa, which made the bars more expensive, and partly due to a change in tastes. The manufacturer's response to rising cocoa prices was to make the bars thinner and this was also proving to be unpopular with consumers. It was against this background that Rowntree-Mackintosh decided to develop a new product line.

How Rowntree-Mackintosh researched the market

Rowntree-Mackintosh spent several years researching the market for bars of chocolate. They did this in a number of ways;

- They looked at existing data available on sales of chocolate products, market shares and consumer trends.
- They used survey information already collected by various market research agencies. These agencies maintain information on people's spending patterns, who buys what and when, what television programmes they are likely to watch, which newspapers they are likely to read, etc. This type of information enabled Rowntree-Mackintosh to *target* the groups of consumers who were most likely to buy a new line in chocolate.
- Further research was carried out on existing brands to find out why people bought them, what made them switch brands and their attitude towards advertising claims.
- Rowntree-Mackintosh, together with their advertising agency, J Walter Thompson, came up with five new *product concepts*. These were tested on four different groups of consumers. Consumers tasted each new product and looked at *mock ups* of the type of advertising that would go with the *product image*. Four out of the five ideas were very rapidly rejected but there was considerable interest in the remaining product. This product was called Rations and was a thick, sustaining bar which was associated with open-air activities. The advertising image showed pictures of mountaineers and used slogans such as, 'When you've got to keep going'.

- Although market research showed that consumers liked Rations it also showed they did not like the name. Several alternative names were thought up, together with different wrapper designs. These were again tested by market research and eventually the name of Yorkie was chosen.
- Finally, a range of advertisements was tested on consumers in order to select the right *image* for the product. The idea of the long-distance truck driver proved to be the most popular and this formed the basis of the advertising campaign.

The outcome

The Yorkie Bar was launched in 1976 and proved very popular, taking 20% of the market for bars of chocolate. It remains popular 10 years later, but has lost some of its market share to competitors.

exercises

1 Explain what is meant by the following terms:
target market,
product concept,
product image.

2 List the methods of market research used by Rowntree-Mackintosh and their advertising agency and describe the type of information that each method discovered.

3 Why do you think the name 'Rations' was less popular than 'Yorkie'?

4 What product image do you think Rowntree-Mackintosh were trying to create by using the truck driver advertisements?

5 Using the advertising examples below to help you, make a list of the methods and images large firms use in advertising their products, eg sex appeal, well-known personalities, etc.

6 Choose any three examples of advertisements and say who you feel they are targeted at, eg age range, male/female, rich/average income earner etc.

Protecting the consumer

Advertising and techniques of sales promotion are very powerful methods of persuading people to buy goods and services. In the past, there was no legislation or body to stop firms making all types of misleading claims about their products.

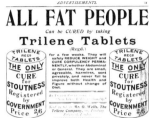

Controls on advertising

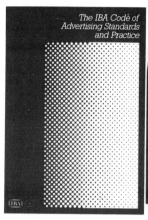

All advertising, apart from television advertising, is monitored and controlled by the Advertising Standards Authority. The ASA makes sure that the British Code of Advertising Practice, drawn up by various representatives of the media, is carried out. The Independent Broadcasting Association (IBA) does the same for radio and television advertising. Advertisements are supposed to be *legal*, *decent*, *honest* and *truthful*.

People who feel that an advertisement breaks this code can complain to the ASA and the offending advertisement will be investigated. The ASA can recommend that an advertisement be withdrawn if it considers that it is breaking the code.

The IBA is sometimes regarded as being more effective as advertisements are vetted *before* they appear on television, whilst the ASA only responds to complaints *after* they appear, by which time the damage may be done.

There is much debate as to what is regarded as being offensive. Are advertisements which show women or men in particular roles offensive? Should advertisements which are directly aimed at children be banned?

A toyshop in your living-room

NIGEL WILLMOTT reports on a disturbing trend in children's television programmes.

BILL BUTCHER

THE Child Poverty Action Group last week called for television advertising of toys to be investigated and possibly more tightly regulated.

Their demands are timely, for in the lead up to Christmas, parents have been pressurised even more than usual to buy toys for their children. The largest influence is television—not just the advertisements, but also the programmes themselves, which are often based on a toy product.

Although the broadcasting authorities have taken some steps to meet these worries, current children's programmes and advertising suggest that the broadcasters' own rules are being broken in spirit, if not in the letter :

■ Bought-in American cartoon series, where effective editorial control lies with the toy manufacturers, questions the basic principle of British public service broadcasting—that advertising and editorial are separate.

■ The level of advertising on both TV-am and Children's ITV seems close to exceeding the IBA's guidelines.

■ Despite strict regulations on children's advertising, there is still misunderstanding.

Toy advertising has been particularly important to TV-am, helping to save it from financial crisis in its first year. Earlier this year the company decided, after discussions with the IBA, to cut toy advertising as a proportion of total advertising volume from 20 per cent to 17.5 per cent next year and to 15 per cent in 1988.

However, a recent edition of the Saturday morning 'The Wide-Awake Club,' the main vehicle for toy advertising, showed 14 minutes of advertising between 7.30 and 9.25 am, and, if the preceding commercial break was included, 15 minutes in two hours. Of the 45 advertisements in that two hours, 35 were for toys. Again, on children's ITV on 4 December between 4 pm and 5 pm, there were 7½ minutes of advertisements, and of 16 advertisements, 12 were for toys or games. The IBA says there should be a maximum of seven minutes of advertising in any clock hour.

The advertisements themselves, disturbing to many parents, are, in fact, to be reviewed by the IBA's Advertising Advisory Committee when it discusses children's advertising next month.

While sex role stereotyping is not dealt with in the IBA's code on advertising standards, virtually without exception, boys are shown with action or construction toys and girls with kitchen or cuddly toys. Next month's IBA meeting will look at 'over-emotional' appeals and 'fantasy' situations in a number of American-made advertisements.

The 'toy-linked' programmes —such as 'He-Man,' 'Transformers,' 'My Little Pony,' 'Care Bears' and 'Mask' — stem directly from the de-regulation of broadcasting in America.

In 1969, when toy maker Mattel, together with the ABC network developed a series based on Mattel's Hot Wheels toys, the Federal Communications Commission banned it. In 1983, when toy manufacturers tried again, the FCC accepted their arguments. As a result, most other kinds of children's programming have now been driven off the screens of the American networks.

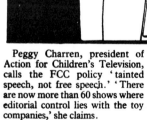

Peggy Charren, president of Action for Children's Television, calls the FCC policy 'tainted speech, not free speech.' 'There are now more than 60 shows where editorial control lies with the toy companies,' she claims.

While Britain does not yet suffer such problems, the influence of the toy manufacturers, particularly the American ones, is important. Hasbro, market leader in the British toy market, had its 'Transformers' running earlier this year on TV-am. Mattel is second in the market, and currently has 'Mask' on TV-am and 'Inspector Gadget' on children's ITV.

Earlier this year the IBA warned ITV companies not to run too many toy-linked series at any one time. It also ruled that advertisements for toys related to programmes should not be shown on the same channel on the same day.

Traditionally, British TV has kept the separation between advertisements and programmes as wide apart as possible. Last year for example the IBA banned a 'My Little Pony' series because it was set to run too close to an advertising campaign. Yet many British parents, especially with an eye on American TV de-regulation, are already very concerned. That concern will grow if British TV goes down a de-regulated path.

1 Why is the Child Poverty Action group concerned about toy advertising?
2 Why might the IBA be reluctant to reduce toy advertising?
3 How might the 'Wide Awake Club' have broken the IBA's guidelines on advertising?
4 What are *toy-linked* programmes? Why is there concern about these types of programmes?
5 Discuss whether or not toy-linked programmes should be banned.

AUSTIN ROVER GROUP LTD
Canley Road
Canley
Coventry CV5 6QX

Agency: DFS Dorland Ltd

(Previous complaints upheld during last 12 months: 2)

Complaints from: Kingston; Ayr

Basis of Complaint: Two members of the public objected to a national press advertisement for the Rover 800 Series, and which included the following claim: "It's first and foremost a car to be driven. The 2.5 litre, V6 fuel-injected engine and its twenty four valves see to that. Generating full-blooded power that will take you to over 130mph before you know it. But the real excitement comes in the way the Sterling handles that power". The complainants objected that the advertisement encouraged and condoned driving at speeds which are both dangerous and illegal. (B.2.2; B.19)

Conclusion: Complaints upheld. The advertisers were advised that the copy approach went beyond what is permitted under the Code in that the description of the speed capability of the vehicle and the presentation of the information was unduly emotive; furthermore it suggested that the driver could experience the direct effect of such speed. The advertisers were asked to ensure that future advertisements suggested neither that it was permissible nor acceptable to drive at speeds in excess of the legal limit.

BRISTOL HIPPODROME
The Centre
Bristol BS1 4UZ

Agency: EAP

Complaint from: Portishead, Avon

Basis of Complaint: A member of the public objected to a local press advertisement for the show "Allo, Allo" which gave details of ticket bookings and which claimed "Monday night 2 for the price of 1". The complainant, who made enquiries about the offer, was advised that tickets were no longer available for Monday night. The complainant therefore questioned the continued appearance of the claim. (B.14.2)

Conclusion: The advertisers stated that when they were aware that all tickets had been sold they had been unable to stop the appearance of a further advertisement and at their request an editorial article had appeared to that effect. They added that a large number of initial reservations had limited the availability of tickets but when reservations were not later confirmed and paid for, over 20 tickets were released on the opening night and were sold at the two for one concession. The Authority considered the advertisers to have acted reasonably in the circumstances.

---

exercise 1 Explain the background to each case and say why the complaint was either upheld or rejected by the ASA.

The government and consumer protection

The consumer was given very little protection against unscrupulous traders in the early part of this century. There was some protection given against being sold short measure and dangerous goods but most legislation came in the 1960s and 1970s. There is now a whole range of legislation designed to protect the consumer and only the more important ones are listed below.

Acts

Sale of Goods Act, 1979

The sale of a good from one person to another is a contract between those two people. The good must be fit for the purpose it is sold for. Any defects in the good must be pointed out at the time the good is sold. (This also applies to goods bought in sales at reduced prices.) Goods should stand up to normal wear; shoes, for example, should not fall to pieces the first time they are worn.

Goods must match the description of them given. A shirt, described as 100% pure cotton, must not contain any nylon (see also Trade Descriptions Act below).

The Act only covers sales from a business — private sales are not covered.

Trade Descriptions Act, 1963

Traders must give an accurate description of their goods or services. Beefburgers described as '100% beef' must not contain anything else.

Unsolicited Goods and Services Act, 1971

Under this Act, a person does not have to pay for goods and services which have not been asked for. If you receive through the post a good which has not been requested, you do not need to return it or pay for it. If the good is not collected after a period of six months the good becomes yours. This period of time is reduced to 28 days if you write to the firm asking them to come and collect it.

Weights and Measures Act, 1963

It is illegal to sell goods which weigh less than the amount stated on the packaging or in an advertisement. Pre-packed goods must show both the weight of the product and the unit weight (weight per pound).

Prices Act, 1974

Prices must not be displayed in a misleading way. Sale prices which show a reduction must have been offered for sale at the higher price for 28 days in the past six months. This is to prevent a shop from artificially raising the price of a product for a day and then reducing it to make it look a real bargain in the sale.

Restaurants must clearly display a menu with prices and this must include VAT and any service charges.

Consumer Credit Acts 1974, 1980, 1985

These Acts cover all goods and services bought on credit up to £15 000. The main points are:

● Customers must be given full information on the credit sale, including the Annual Percentage Rate of interest (APR) being charged, the cash price of the item and the total credit price.

● A customer who signs a credit agreement at home has 14 days to change their mind and cancel the agreement. (This is to avoid people being 'pressurised' by door-to-door salesmen into taking on agreements.) This does not apply to agreements signed on trade premises.

Fair Trading Act, 1973

This set up the Office of Fair Trading and the post of Director General of Fair Trading. The OFT does not deal with complaints from consumers but suggests new laws on trading and can take action against firms who are regarded as engaging in unfair trading practices. This might include agreements between firms on prices or restrictions on competition. The OFT can also ask the Monopolies and Mergers Commission to investigate take-overs and mergers if it feels that they are against the interest of the public.

Unfair Contract Terms Act, 1980

This Act prevents firms from avoiding their responsibilities by writing certain clauses into their contracts. For example, a dry cleaner cannot avoid paying compensation if items are damaged, even though he may have a sign up in his shop which states that he does not accept liability for loss or damage to items during cleaning. All *disclaimers* must be *reasonable* to be acceptable.

Food and Drugs Act, 1955

This Act makes it illegal to offer food for sale which is 'unfit for human consumption'.

How to complain

- The seller is responsible if a good proves to be faulty or not fit for the purpose it is sold for. The customer must take the good back to the shop where it was purchased and not go to the manufacturer.
- If the seller accepts that the good is faulty he must offer the customer all of his money back. The customer does not have to accept a replacement good, the offer of a repair, or a credit note.
- If the shop refuses to accept responsibility, the customer may wish to seek help from the Citizen's Advice Bureau (see page 196). The customer may be advised to take the matter up with the firm direct or to contact a trade organisation, if the firm is a member of one.
- If these courses of action fail to bring a satisfactory result, then the customer will need to take the matter to court. If the value of the good is less than £500 the customer can take the matter to the *Small Claims Court*. This is much cheaper than going to the County Court and the customer can pursue his case without the need for a solicitor.

Do you know your rights?

In each case below state what your rights are and name the appropriate course of action to be taken. Mention any Acts involved in the case.

1 You buy a pair of jeans in a sale. When you get them home you find that there is a fault in some of the stitching. You take them back to the shop but the manager refuses to give you your money back, pointing to a clear sign which says 'Sale goods not returnable'.
2 You receive some charity Christmas cards through the post. There is a note inside asking you to purchase them or to return them to the charity within fourteen days.
3 You are over 18 and have just signed an HP agreement to buy a motorcycle. After signing the agreement in the shop you have second thoughts about it and decide to cancel the agreement. You were given the full facts about how much it would cost you at the time of signing.
4 You buy a jumper at Marks and Spencer. When you get home you find it is the wrong size.

5 You open a tin of tuna fish and find a dead fly inside.

Independent help for the consumer

The British Standards Institute (BSI)

This awards the *Kitemark* to goods which are tested and come up to British Standards. These standards lay down such things as the safety factors, quality of materials, and thickness and strength, for a large number of products.

British Electrotechnical Approvals Board (BEAB)

This is similar to BSI but deals only with domestic electrical equipment such as televisions, fires, hair dryers and electric blankets. The BEAB label shows that the item has passed the very strict standards laid down in the test. Some items, such as electric blankets, must pass the BEAB test to be sold in the UK.

BEAB
Approved
via CCA

Citizen's Advice Bureau (CABs)

These receive some Government and local authority support but remain independent. They are staffed partly by volunteers and partly by paid employees. They give free advice on most matters including consumer problems. They will advise on the courses of action available and may take the matter up informally with the shop or firm concerned in the dispute. Some local authorities have a specialist Consumer Advice Centre which concentrates purely on consumer problems.

Trade associations

Many industries have their own trade associations which lay down codes of practice for their members. Examples of these include the Association of British Travel Agents (ABTA) and the Motor Agents Association (MAA). Consumers can make complaints to the trade association if they feel a firm is breaking their code of practice.

The Consumers Association

This is a completely private organisation which is financed from members' subscriptions. The Consumers Association publishes *Which?* magazine each month which includes tests on products and recommends 'Best Buys'. The Consumers Association also acts as a pressure group on firms and the Government when it feels that products are unsatisfactory or consumers have been treated unfairly.

The Trading Standards Department and Environmental Health Departments

These are maintained by local authorities to check on such matters as weights and measures, local trade practices and public health.

Nationalised Industry Consumer Councils

These investigate complaints made by consumers about the nationalised industries (see page 210).

Transport

The importance of transport in business

Transport is included in this unit because it is an important part of selling, but it is equally important for other areas of business activity. Transport is used in business for:

- Transporting materials and components to the factory.
- Moving finished goods from the factory to the wholesaler.
- Transporting goods from the wholesaler to the retailer.
- Workers getting to work and attending meetings and conferences.
- Transporting documents.

Types of transport

Transport can be divided into two kinds:

- Internal transport within the UK (Road, Rail, Canals, Coastal Shipping, Air and Pipelines).
- External transport between the UK and other countries (air and sea)

Within the UK, roads are by far the most important method of transporting goods. Roads have increased their share of freight carried in the last 20 years mainly at the expense of rail.

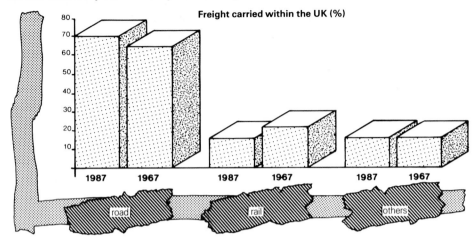

Freight carried within the UK (%)

Which type of transport?

In deciding upon a method of transport, businesses have to take account of a number of factors:

- *Cost* This normally depends upon the distance a good needs to be sent, and its weight and size.
- *Time* Whether a good needs to arrive at its destination the next day or can wait for three weeks.
- *The nature of the good* Whether it is fragile, or perishable, or of very high value, or whether it requires specialised transport, as in the case of dangerous chemicals.

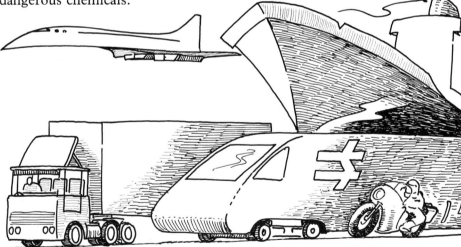

Road

Road transport accounts for over 90% of passenger traffic and 70% of freight carried within the UK. Some firms have their own fleet of lorries, others use road-haulage companies. The nature of some goods means that specialist vehicles are required, eg milk, livestock, petrol.

Advantages

- Very flexible. The extensive road network means that goods can be delivered from door to door with the minimum of handling.
- A range of specialist vehicles to suit all needs.
- Relatively cheap for both goods and passengers because of low overheads compared with alternatives.
- Fastest method for most goods and many passenger journeys.

Disadvantages

- Restrictions on weight and width.
- Congestion in towns and cities.
- Journeys may be affected by bad weather conditions.

Rail

In the past 20 years, rail has been losing its share of both the freight and passenger markets. The number of lines have been reduced but the speed of service on inter-city routes has improved and there has been some increase in the businessman trade. Rail is almost totally controlled by the Government through British Rail.

Advantages

- Faster on some journeys for passengers than road, eg Newcastle to London (300 miles) in three hours.
- Less strain than driving; allows work to be done on journey.
- May be cheaper for certain regular, bulky loads, such as coal, where special rates can be negotiated with British Rail.
- Fast for small items which can be sent by passenger train (see Red Star Service, Unit 10 page 122).

Disadvantages

- Less flexible than road because routes and times are fixed.
- Often slower and more expensive because goods and passengers need to get to a station to start their journey, and at the end of their journey from the station to their final destination.

An airfreight service

Air

In the past twenty years air has increased its share of passenger and freight transport both within the UK and overseas. Even so, it still only accounts for a small part of passenger and freight transport within the UK compared with countries such as the USA.

Advantages

- Fast for long journeys.
- Safe for expensive or fragile goods.
- Some freight may now be more cheaply sent overseas by air than sea because it requires less specialist packing, and less insurance, as the journey time is shorter.

Disadvantages

- Expensive for heavy, bulky goods.
- Not able to carry certain very large items.
- For short journeys, the time taken getting to and from airports may increase overall journey time and make it slower than alternatives.

Sea and inland waterways

The Baltic Exchange

Inland waterways (rivers and canals) are now far less important than they were 100 years ago. Sea has remained important for overseas trade although it has lost out recently to air freight.

Vessels can be chartered (hired) on the Baltic Exchange. These ships transport cargoes on single journeys and do not have regular routes. *Cargo liners* have regular routes and either carry general cargoes or specialise in a particular commodity, such as oil or timer.

Advantages

- Can carry any cargo whatever its size or weight.
- Normally cheaper for very heavy or bulky goods.
- Can offer specialist facilities for particular goods.

Disadvantages

- Slow, and so sometimes expensive.
- Goods often require specialist packing.
- Goods more easily damaged because they are in transit longer.
- Limited by port facilities or availability of canals and inland waterways.

Containerisation

Containerisation has been a very important development for freight transportation in recent years. A container is a standard metal box which can be packed at the factory and sealed. If it is going overseas it can be checked and approved by customs and the various documents can be prepared in advance. The containers are designed to fit lorries, freightliner trains and ships, so they can be moved from one to the other without unpacking.

Advantages of using containers

- Saves time — less packing and unpacking.
- Less likelihood of theft of stock because the container is sealed throughout its journey.
- Less chance of damage during transit because goods are handled less frequently.
- The inside of the container may be specially designed to cope with particular goods.

exercise   For each situation given, select the best method (or methods) of transport and give reasons to support your choice.

1 A businessman in Leeds needs to get to an important conference in Central London.
2 Medical equipment from Cambridge is urgently needed in Ethiopia.
3 Very large quantities of cement need to be regularly sent from Kent to Birmingham.
4 Dangerous chemicals need to be sent from the north-east of England to Manchester.
5 A large textile machine needs to be imported from Australia to Lancashire.

Summary of key words and ideas

- Products have a marketing *life-cycle* of research and development, introduction, growth, maturity (saturation), decline and obsolescence.
- It is normally only in the mature stage of the cycle that total costs of production start to be covered.
- Firms use a variety of methods of *market research* including the use of existing information, as well as surveys and test marketing.
- *Target market* The people that a product is aimed at according to age, sex and income.
- *Product Concept* The idea for a new product and the image which the manufacturers are trying to create for it.
- *Product Image* The view manufacturers and advertisers wish consumers to have of their product.
- *Consumer protection* is necessary to safeguard the buyer from being misled by advertising or sold faulty or dangerous products.
- The *IBA* supervises advertising on television and radio through a code of practice. The *ASA* does the same for all other forms of advertising.
- The consumer is protected by legislation and independent consumer bodies.
- A sale of a good implies a contract between the seller and the buyer.
- Businesses will take account of a range of factors such as cost, speed, security and the nature of the goods to be transported when selecting an appropriate form of transportation.

Suggestions for coursework

1 Choose a product bought by your colleagues. Carry out market research to find out why they buy it, what makes them choose a particular brand, etc. On the basis of this information, design three new product concepts. Carry out further market research to select the one which is likely to be the most successful. Prepare for a final launch by refining your product and its advertising.

2 Prepare a quiz on consumer protection and test it on different groups of people by age and sex to find out their knowledge and understanding of their rights. Visit a Citizens' Advice Bureau to find out the consumer area where they receive most requests for help.

3 Select two different firms and find out what methods of transportation they use and why these particular methods have been selected.

4 Carry out consumer research on supermarket plastic carrier bags. How much do they cost? How strong and/or attractive are they?

5 Record a variety of TV or radio advertisements. Analyze them in terms of when they appeared, length, method of selling, etc.

Test questions

1 Complete the following for the life cycle of a product:
Research and Development ......? Growth .....? Maturity
(saturation) .....? Obselescence .....?

2 Name four ways in which a firm might try to make its brand of a
product appear to be different from that of a rival.

3 Your brand of soap is losing some of its share of the market to a
rival. Describe two methods of product promotion you could use to
try to regain your share of the market.

4 'Before the launch of their new car, Ford spent two years carefully
researching the market. They looked at existing data as well as
carrying out their own market research. They felt that it was very
important to select the correct image for their new product and that
the advertising conveyed the correct message to the consumer.'

   a What is meant by *the launch* of a product?

   b Explain how Ford would go about researching the market for a
   new car.

   c Give an example of an *image* that Ford might want to create for a
   new car.

5 Describe four different ways in which the consumer is protected.

6 Advertising on television is controlled by a code of practice.

   a What body attempts to see that the code of practice is carried
   out?

   b Give an example of an advertisement that might break the code of
   practice.

7 'When a good is sold there is a contract between the seller and the
buyer even though there may be nothing written down.'

   a What does a contract mean in this case?

   b Name three legal obligations which are placed on the seller.

8 Name three things a person must be told when buying a good on
credit.

9 a What does the 'Kitemark' tell the consumer?

   b Describe one other label a product might have to help a
   consumer.

10 Describe two ways in which the Consumers Association helps
consumers.

11 A firm in Glasgow has just completed making a consignment of large
steel pipes for a firm in London. Name two methods of transport the
firm could use. Select the one you feel is the best and give your
reasons for the choice.

12 Name a product which would normally be transported by air and
give the reasons why this is the case.

Extension questions

1 'Advertising raises a firm's fixed costs but helps to increase its revenue'. Explain what this sentence means.

2 'Containerisation has lowered the unit costs of transporting goods.'
   a Explain how the container system works.
   b How has it lowered unit costs?

3 Study the graph below and answer the following questions:
   a Why does the cost per kilometre of both road and rail transport fall with the distance of the journey?
   b Why is rail transport per kilometre more expensive than road over short distances?

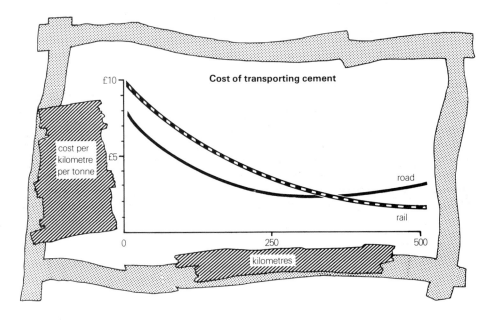

Section IV

The public sector

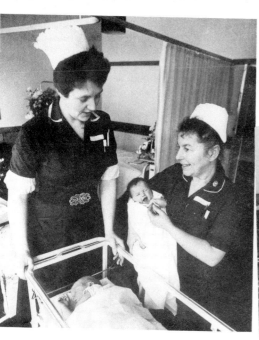

Unit 15 State and local government enterpris

aims At the end of this unit you should understand:

▶ What is meant by the public sector.
▶ The importance of the public sector in the UK economy.
▶ The aims of the public sector and how they differ from the aims of the private sector.
▶ How the public sector is controlled and managed.
▶ How the public sector is financed.
▶ What is meant by privatisation.
▶ What is meant by social costs.

What is the public sector?

The public sector consists of all those businesses which are directly owned by the state (the Government) or by a local authority (a council). All other businesses are in the private sector.

(*Note* Public companies, such as Barclays Bank, or Shell Oil, are in the private sector)

exercise Place the following business activities into two groups under the headings of *public enterprise* and *private enterprise*:

The importance of the public sector

In the UK, just under half of all economic activity is produced by the public sector. Approximately 30% of the working population is directly employed by the state or by local authorities and many more people are indirectly employed, (eg private building firms constructing council houses). The public sector consists of:

● Services provided by the State (National Health Service, Defence, etc.)
● Nationalised industries and public corporations (British Steel, BBC, British Coal, etc.)
● Local authority services (education, street cleaning, recreational facilities, etc.)

Aims of public enterprise

The main aim of the private sector is to make a profit; nationalised industries are also meant to make a profit, some make very large profits (as with British Gas, before it was sold to the private sector), whilst others, such as British Steel, have made large losses. But profit is not the main aim of the public sector. There is a variety of aims, and these are best seen by looking at the reasons for public sector enterprise.

Reasons for public sector enterprise

- To provide a service where the private sector does not make provision because it is unprofitable, eg sewerage, defence, uneconomic railway lines, the care of the sick and the elderly.
- To provide a basic level of service in areas which are regarded as being socially very important, eg education, health, fire protection.
- To control more easily an industry where the nature of the good or service means that it is in the hands of one supplier, (known as a *monopoly*), eg the Post Office, electricity, British Rail
- To assist an industry which is facing severe economic problems. This was the case with industries such as steel and coal which faced a rapid decline after 1945 because of a loss of their markets.

The reasons for an industry being in the public sector are often political. In recent years some industries, such as gas, telecommunications and even rubbish collection, have been put into the private sector. There is considerable argument as to whether they are best in the public or the private sector.

case study

Should we privatise the National Health Service?

In the US there is very little public enterprise. Many of the jobs done by the public sector in the UK are carried out by the private sector in the US. Rubbish collection, electricity and water supply are very often in the hands of private companies in the US. There is no National Health Service in the US. The patient is charged a fee when s/he visits the doctor and all medical care has to be paid for. A stay in a hospital costs about £100 a day, and that does not include any treatment! A broken limb could cost £1000 or more and major operations could easily cost £10 000. To help pay for this, Americans take out insurance cover. This is expensive and increases with the age of the person and their medical record. As with car insurance, there is a no-claims discount for people with good medical records.

Some people in the UK would like to see a system for health care similar to that of the US. They argue that taxes would be lower and health care would be more efficient, with less waiting time and a better standard of service.

questions

1 Make a list of arguments both for and against having only private medical care.
2 How is the National Health Service paid for in the UK?
3 How is medical care paid for in the US?
4 Do you think a totally private medical system would be cheaper or more expensive than the National Health Service? Explain your answer.
5 Would a private medical system be more efficient than a public one? Explain your answer.
6 Who might benefit and who might suffer if the National Health Service was abolished and replaced by a totally private system?

The idea of social costs

One argument often used to support public enterprise is that of *social costs*. Social costs are all the costs which a particular decision imposes on society. A decision to build a new stretch of motorway, for example, will not only have private costs, such as the cost of the land and the construction costs, but will also have social costs in terms of the noise and other forms of environmental damage it may inflict on the area.

It is argued that the private sector only takes account of private costs when it is making a decision, whilst the public sector is able to take account of both private and social costs. This is illustrated in the following case study.

---

case study   ## Should the Barton line close?

Barton is a seaside town with a population of 50 000. It is at the end of a railway line linking it to the City of Runswick, 25 miles away. The road link between Barton and Runswick is poor and is less direct than the railway because there is currently no road crossing of the Barr estuary. The rail link currently makes an annual loss of £500 000 and its future is under consideration.

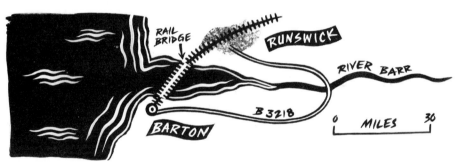

A group of residents, hearing that the line was under threat, formed the 'Save the Barton Line Society'. These were the points they put forward to British Rail in favour of keeping the line open:

- Closure of the line would mean increased journey times by road. Many people commute to Runswick and the increased journey time by road would make this very difficult. This could add to the already high unemployment in the area.
- Many tourists and day trippers come to Barton by rail and closure of the line would mean a decline in the tourist trade and a loss of jobs in the tourist industry.
- The cost of improving the road system would be equal to the current losses on the rail link for at least five years.

---

questions   1 What are the social costs of closing the rail link?
2 Why would a private company close the line?
3 Why might British Rail keep the line open?

Public corporations and nationalised industries

Note Nationalised industries are those industries which used to be in private hands and were taken over by the state, eg, British Rail, British Coal, the Central Electricity Generating Board. Not all public corporations are nationalised industries; some have always been in state hands, eg, the Post Office and the British Broadcasting Corporation.

Organisation and control of a public corporation: the Central Electricity Generating Board (CEGB).

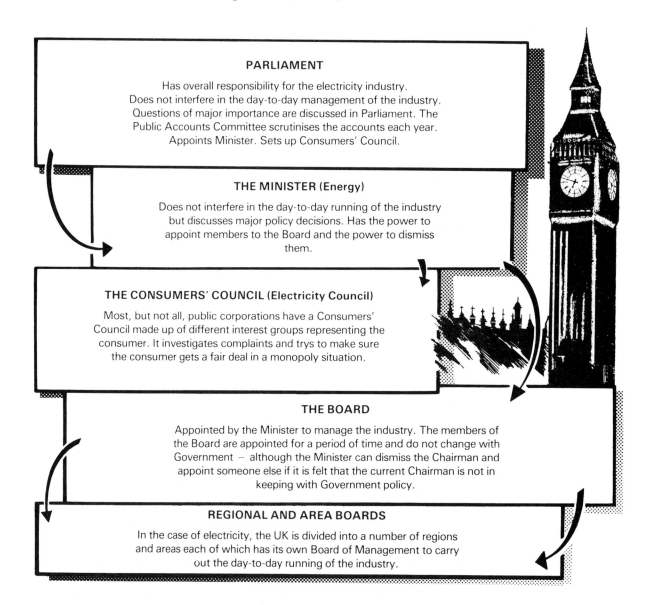

PARLIAMENT

Has overall responsibility for the electricity industry. Does not interfere in the day-to-day management of the industry. Questions of major importance are discussed in Parliament. The Public Accounts Committee scrutinises the accounts each year. Appoints Minister. Sets up Consumers' Council.

THE MINISTER (Energy)

Does not interfere in the day-to-day running of the industry but discusses major policy decisions. Has the power to appoint members to the Board and the power to dismiss them.

THE CONSUMERS' COUNCIL (Electricity Council)

Most, but not all, public corporations have a Consumers' Council made up of different interest groups representing the consumer. It investigates complaints and trys to make sure the consumer gets a fair deal in a monopoly situation.

THE BOARD

Appointed by the Minister to manage the industry. The members of the Board are appointed for a period of time and do not change with Government – although the Minister can dismiss the Chairman and appoint someone else if it is felt that the current Chairman is not in keeping with Government policy.

REGIONAL AND AREA BOARDS

In the case of electricity, the UK is divided into a number of regions and areas each of which has its own Board of Management to carry out the day-to-day running of the industry.

(*Note* There is no one way in which Public Corporations have to be organised, but the CEGB is typical of many nationalised industries.)

Financing public corporations

Public corporations obtain their finance from four main sources:

- *Grants and loans from the Government.* This is financed from taxation and government borrowing. Money is normally loaned on the basis of it being paid back with interest, but in some cases, where the Corporation continues to make large losses, the Government has to 'write off' outstanding loans.
- *Direct borrowing from the public.* Nationalised industries can sell stock or borrow in other ways, from the public and financial institutions. The Government guarantees the interest and repayment.
- *Grants and loans from other public corporations.* Some public corporations make large profits and these are used to help finance loss-making corporations or major investment projects.
- *Fees.* These are the main source of finance for the BBC.

TELEVISION LICENCE   MONOCHROME ONLY ★/MONOCHROME & COLOUR ★ General Form

This licence expires on the last day of .... 19 .....

WIRELESS TELEGRAPHY ACT 1949

Financial management of public corporations

Public corporations are meant to be run so that they 'break even' and make enough profit to cover future investment. Nationalised industries are expected to make a return on any investment equal to what would be expected if they were in the private sector. As indicated earlier, some make very large profits, and some make very large losses. When a very large profit is made, the corporation either invests it, loans it to other industries or it may give rebates to consumers. This occurred when British Gas was state owned — consumers were given a rebate on part of their gas bill when it made an exceptionally high profit.

When a public corporation makes a loss, it has to be met from Government funds — either through taxation or through borrowing.

Public corporations which are making large losses often need to borrow, not only to cover their losses, but also to help with investment to modernise the industry in the future.

Privatisation

Privatisation is the selling of a public sector enterprise to the private sector. This is normally done by inviting the public to buy shares in the enterprise which is being sold off. This was the case with British Telecom, British Gas, the Trustee Savings Bank, and British Airways.

TSB GROUP plc
(Registered in Scotland No. 95000)

OFFER FOR SALE

by

LAZARD BROTHERS & CO., LIMITED

on behalf of the

TRUSTEE SAVINGS BANKS CENTRAL BOARD

of up to 1,495,830,450 ordinary shares of 25p each
at 100p per share
of which 50p is payable now
and 50p is payable on 8th September, 1987

British Gas

Share Offer

by

N M Rothschild & Sons Limited

on behalf of

The Secretary of State for Energy

In all these cases, the shares on offer were considerably oversubscribed — more people wanted to purchase them than there were available for sale. This caused the share price to rise rapidly when dealing opened on the Stock Exchange. Shareholders, in the case of British Telecom and British Gas, were offered vouchers to help pay bills as well as interest on their shares and the chance to make a capital gain.

The privatisation of British Gas was the largest ever *flotation* of a company in the UK. 4 025 500 000 shares were offered for sale at a price of 135p per share. The shares were well oversubscribed when applications closed in December 1986.

The case for privatisation

Privatisation is very much a political issue. The arguments put forward in favour of privatisation include:

- Industry is more efficiently managed in the private sector.
- Sale of public corporations raises money for the Government which would otherwise need to be raised through borrowing or taxation.
- The privatisation of an industry makes it more subject to competition and this helps to make it more efficient.
- It is not the job of Government to run industries which can quite easily be managed by the private sector.

The arguments against privatisation

- It is debatable whether the private sector is more efficient than the public sector.
- The corporations which have been sold off were all highly profitable ones and their sale has resulted in a long-term loss of revenue to the Government.
- The sale to the private sector has not increased competition. Public monopolies have simply become private monopolies over which the Government has less control.

Local authorities

England and Wales (outside Greater London) are divided into 53 large county authorities. The county authorities are further divided into 369 smaller district authorities. Greater London is divided into 32 boroughs.

Scotland is divided into nine regions which are subdivided into 53 districts. Northern Ireland has 26 district councils but some services, such as education, housing and roads, are supplied centrally.

What do local authorities do?

Local authorities must, by law, supply certain services, including education, refuse collection, and fire and police services. These are called *mandatory services*. Other services, such as leisure facilities, are at the discretion of the local authority.

A council may supply these services directly or put them out to *tender* by private firms. Some councils have private companies to collect refuse, clean the streets and supply school meals.

exercises

1 List all the services which are provided by your local authority.
2 Your local authority has put school meals out to tender. The contract is awarded to a private company who will produce the meals centrally and reheat them in microwave ovens in the schools. The Council will pay the company for any free meals which are provided.
   a List the arguments for and against awarding the contract to the private firm.
   b Who will gain and who will lose from the decision?

How do local authorities finance the provision of services?

- *Fees* from users (admission charges, market rents, etc.)
- *Rates* from private housing, shops and factories.
- *Block grants* from the Government out of central taxation.
- Borrowing by selling *local authority bonds* which carry a guaranteed fixed rate of interest.
- *Lotteries* Members of the public are invited to buy tickets in a draw, with the chance to win cash prizes.

Approximately half of the finance comes through rates and a further quarter to one third comes from the Government block grant.

How are rates calculated?

A rateable value is fixed for each property in a local authority area. The amount of the rateable value will depend upon:

- What the property is used for (housing, shop, factory, etc).
- The size of the property.
- The facilities the property has. (Number of rooms, garage, etc).
- Where the property is. A house in a select part of town will be more highly rated than one next to an industrial estate. A shop in a new precinct in the centre of a town will be more highly rated than one in the suburbs.
- All of the rateable values added together gives the rateable value for the whole local authority area. This tells the Council how much each £1 of rates will raise.
- The Council calculates how much revenue it requires from the rates and fixes an amount in the pound. If the rate was fixed at 150p in the pound and the rateable value of the whole authority was £200 million, then the amount raised would be £300 million (£200 million × 1.5). Someone who had a house with a rateable value of £400 would pay £600 in rates (£400 × 1.5).

exercises

Midshire County Council fix their rate at 200p in the pound.

1 How much would a person owning a shop with a rateable value of £600 pay in rates?
2 What is the rateable value of a house if someone pays £500 in rates?
3 The rate is expected to raise £500 million for Midshire. What is the total rateable value of Midshire?

Note In 1989, the government plans to abolish rates and replace them with a community charge or poll tax. This will be a fixed amount charged on each person over the age of 18. Some people, such as those on very low incomes, will pay a reduced amount or be exempt altogether.

case study   Wessex County Council

The diagram shows how Wessex County Council raised its finance and how this was spent last year.

1 What percentage of their revenue came from ratepayers?
2 What percentage of their revenue came from central government?
3 What was over half the revenue used to provide?
4 What would be provided by Social Services?
5 The Jones family have three children, aged 14, 16 and 18. The eldest is at university. The Jones family live in a three-bedroom, semi-detached house and own a car.

Mr and Mrs Smith are pensioners living on their own in a four-bedroom, detached house. They do not own a car.

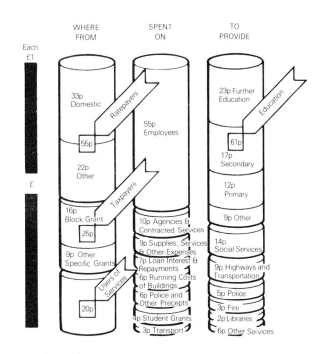

WHERE FROM   SPENT ON   TO PROVIDE

Each £1

WHERE FROM: 33p Domestic — Ratepayers — 55p; 22p Other; 16p Block Grant — Taxpayers — 25p; 9p Other Specific Grants — Users of Services — 20p

SPENT ON: 55p Employees; 10p Agencies & Contracted Services; 9p Supplies, Services & Other Expenses; 7p Loan Interest & Repayments; 6p Running Costs of Buildings; 6p Police and Other Precepts; 4p Student Grants; 3p Transport

TO PROVIDE: 23p Further Education — Education — 61p; 17p Secondary; 12p Primary; 9p Other; 14p Social Services; 9p Highways and Transportation; 5p Police; 3p Fire; 2p Libraries; 6p Other Services

a What services provided by Wessex County Council would both households use?
b Which services would be used by the Jones household and not by the Smiths?
c Which services might be used by the Smiths and not by the Jones family?
d Which household would pay more in rates? (Explain your answer.)
e In what way might the rates system be considered as unfair?

extension case study   A new hypermarket for Barchester?

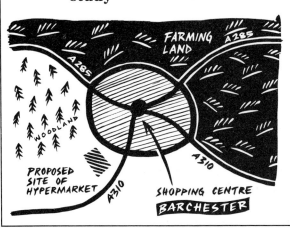

FARMING LAND — A285 — A285 — WOODLAND — PROPOSED SITE OF HYPERMARKET — A310 — A310 — SHOPPING CENTRE BARCHESTER

Barchester is an old and attractive city with a busy shopping area in its centre. AW Mitchell Associates, a property development company, has applied for permission to build a hypermarket on an area of land now owned by the Council. The area of land is on the outskirts of the town and is currently used for recreational purposes. They have offered either to buy the land or to rent it from the Council.

1 List all the costs and all the benefits of allowing the scheme to go ahead.
2 Say whether each of the following people would be in favour or against the scheme, giving reasons for your decision:
  a a shopkeeper in the centre of the city,
  b the chairman of the Barchester Council finance committee,
  c the chairman of the Barchester Council leisure committee,
  d the chairman of the Barchester Council employment committee,
  e a householder living in the city.

Summary of key words and ideas

- The *public sector* consists of all those enterprises which are owned by the state or local authorities.
- *Social costs* are the costs imposed on society by a particular decision.
- The public sector has aims other than the maximisation of profit and may take account of social costs when making decisions. The private sector does not normally take account of social costs because profit is its main aim.
- Public corporations and nationalised industries are answerable to parliament who appoints a Minister and a Board to supervise the running of the industry.
- The Consumer Councils represent the public and look into complaints made about the public corporation.
- *Privatisation* is the sale of public corporations to the private sector.
- *Rates* are taxes on property which are used to finance local authority spending.
- The public sector needs to weigh up all the costs, including social costs, and all the benefits in making decisions on particular projects.

Suggestions for coursework

1 Every local authority must publish information on how it raises its finance and how it spends it. Obtain copies of this information from two councils and compare their finance and expenditure. Try and explain any major variations between the two authorities.
2 Take any major new development project in your area, eg a shopping centre, hypermarket, leisure centre, or industrial estate. Find out as much as you can about it from the Council and local newspapers, eg how much it is costing and how it is being financed. Analyse the costs and benefits of the project. If you had the deciding vote on the Council, would you vote for or against the project? Explain the reasoning behind your decision.
3 Try to obtain details of how the new community charge or 'poll tax' might operate in your area. Carry out a survey to test local residents' reactions to it. Who will be better or worse off as a result of it?

Test questions

1 Name three nationalised industries, one in the primary sector, one in the secondary sector, and one in the tertiary sector of the economy.
2 Give two reasons for state ownership of industry.
3 Briefly describe what each of the following does in connection with a nationalised industry:
Parliament,
the minister responsible for the nationalised industry,
the Consumer Council for the nationalised industry,
the board.
4 Describe two ways in which public corporations raise finance.
5 Describe three important ways in which local authorities obtain finance.
6 Name four important services provided by local authorities.
7 Name four factors which determine the rateable value of a property.
8 The rate in Midshire has been fixed at 180p in the pound. What would be the rates on a property with a rateable value of £500?
9 The Betchington City Council is considering what to do with an area of land near the city centre which has recently become vacant. There are two main proposals:
a a new shopping centre to be developed by a private property company.
b for the Council to purchase the land and build a leisure centre and a car park.
List the advantages and disadvantages of each proposal and say which you would vote for, giving the reasons for your decision.

extension questions

1 Explain why the current system of rates might be regarded as unfair and suggest an alternative method to replace it.
2 What is meant by social costs? Describe two social costs which might result from the closure of a coal pit.
3 Choose any public corporation and put the case for and against its privatisation.
4 Brunton Town Council is currently deciding whether its street cleaning and rubbish collection should be done by a private company or continue to be done by the Council employees. A private company has submitted a tender which is less than the current cost to the Council.
a What is a 'tender'?
b What are the arguments for and against having the work done by a private contractor?

Unit 16   The government and business

aims   At the end of this unit you should understand:

▶   How overall government economic policy affects business.
▶   How particular government measures both aid and control business.

Note   Many of the ways in which government aids and controls business are dealt with in detail in earlier units. This unit provides a summary of the large range of government measures affecting business activity.

Government economic policy and business

The targets

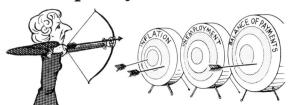

The targets for government economic policy and how much importance is given to each one depends upon which political party is in power. Most political parties would agree on the following objectives:

●   A low rate of inflation (the rate at which prices in general are rising).
●   A low level of unemployment.
●   Growth in the general level of income and wealth through a growing economy.
●   A surplus of exports over imports. *Exports* are goods and services sold abroad. Imports are goods and services bought from overseas.

In order to try to achieve its objectives, government has a number of measures at its disposal including:

●   Changes in taxation, both *direct taxes*, such as income tax, and *indirect taxes*, such as VAT.
●   Increasing or decreasing the amount of public expenditure on such things as old-age pensions, defence, and social services.
●   Increasing or decreasing the amount of money it borrows. Government does not raise all the money it requires through taxes. The difference between its revenue from tax and the amount it spends is financed through borrowing (National Savings, Premium Bonds, etc).
●   *Interest rates*   Government has some influence over the cost of borrowing money. It can also influence the ease with which credit can be obtained.
●   *The Exchange Rate*   This is the rate at which one currency can be changed for another. The Government has some influence over the rate at which the pound can be changed for other currencies.

Taxation

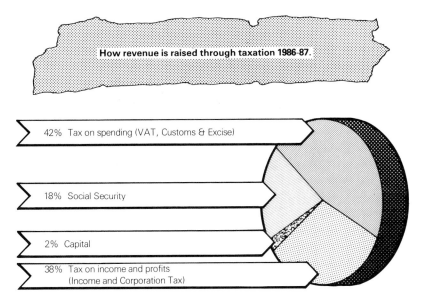

How revenue is raised through taxation 1986-87.

- 42% Tax on spending (VAT, Customs & Excise)
- 18% Social Security
- 2% Capital
- 38% Tax on income and profits (Income and Corporation Tax)

Changes in taxation have both a direct influence and an indirect influence upon business. If government were to increase the tax on petrol, the price of petrol would rise (unless the oil companies paid all of the tax increase themselves). The direct result of this may be that less petrol is bought. The indirect effects may be that the cost of transport rises and that people have less money to spend in general (assuming that they buy some petrol and that there are no other changes in tax or expenditure). The cost of delivering goods and raw materials will increase and this will be passed on to consumers in the form of higher prices.

Kinds of tax

Income tax is paid to the Inland Revenue and is charged on all earnings, including employment, self-employment, interest and rents.

Corporation tax is a tax paid by companies on their profits. Companies are allowed to *offset* tax against any losses they have made.

Value Added Tax (VAT) is a tax paid on most goods and services. It is charged at each stage in production but is passed on to the final consumer.

Customs duties are charged on goods brought into the country.

Excise duties are charged on certain products made in the UK, eg beer, cigarettes, whisky, petrol. About 80% of the price of a packet of cigarettes and over 50% of the price of a gallon of petrol is taken in tax.

Public expenditure

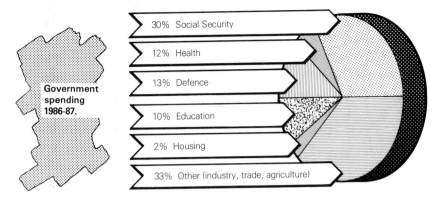

Government spending 1986-87.

- 30% Social Security
- 12% Health
- 13% Defence
- 10% Education
- 2% Housing
- 33% Other (industry, trade, agriculture)

Public expenditure has both direct and indirect effects upon business:

- The level of government spending influences the amount of money people have to spend in general and this in turn affects the demand for the goods and services produced by firms.
- Government spending may have a direct influence on particular businesses. For example, a decision to increase spending on housing will affect the building industry and those firms supplying building materials.

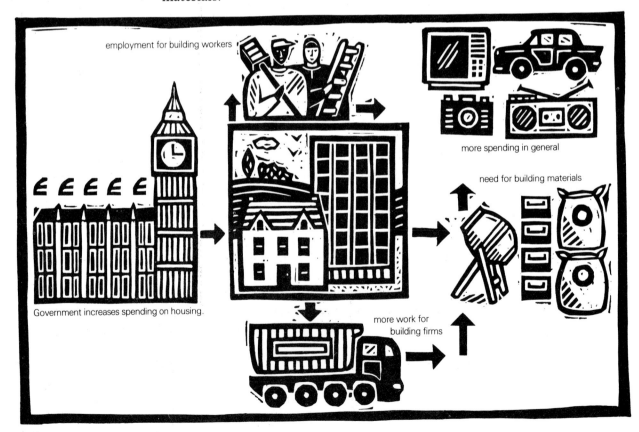

employment for building workers

more spending in general

need for building materials

Government increases spending on housing.

more work for building firms

exercises For each situation given below, produce a diagram similar to the one at the bottom of page 220 to show the possible effects of the change on business:

a Government increases the excise duty on beer.
b Income tax is reduced and VAT on cars is abolished.
c Public expenditure in general is reduced and there is a particular reduction in spending on defence.
d There is a large increase in spending on books, materials and equipment in primary schools and in overall government spending.

Interest rates

The rate of interest is the charge for borrowing money for a period of time. There are lots of different rates of interest and the charge will vary for example between bank loans, hire purchase agreements, credit card sales, and building society mortgages. The rates at which banks loan money will also vary depending upon the type of customer and the size of the loan. Large firms, requiring large loans, can often negotiate lower rates of interest than small borrowers. All these rates of interest are linked together and government has an influence over them. The rate of interest is very important to businesses.

INTEREST RATES **UK HIGH STREET %**	Bank deposit rate : 4.5	Building society mortgage : 11-12.37
	Bank base rate : 10.5	Building society deposit : 6 net
	Bank overdraft : 14 – 16	Finance House rate : 11

A rise in the rate of interest will mean:

- The cost of borrowing money for firms will have increased. This increases their total costs and either results in lower profits or price increases.
- Firms will be more reluctant to take on new borrowing and there may be less investment in new equipment and buildings.
- Firms will find it more difficult to expand by borrowing money.
- Consumers will find it more expensive to buy on credit and there will be less demand for goods and services in general.

The reverse will be true of a fall in interest rates:

- Existing loans will be cheaper, resulting in a fall in total costs.
- Firms may be encouraged to borrow money for new equipment, buildings, and expansion schemes.
- Consumers will find it cheaper to buy on credit, resulting in an increase in demand for goods and services. This effect will be further increased if the mortgage rate falls, allowing people more money to spend on things other than housing.

UK MONEY MARKETS %	7 day	1 month	3 months	6 months
Treasury bills	–	10	$9\frac{5}{8}$	–
Eligible bills	–	$10\frac{1}{32}$	$9\frac{17}{32}$	$9\frac{9}{32}$
Interbank rate	$11\frac{1}{8}$	$10\frac{3}{8}$	$9\frac{15}{16}$	$9\frac{13}{16}$
Sterling CDs	–	$10\frac{3}{8}$	$9\frac{7}{8}$	$9\frac{11}{16}$
Local Authority Deposits	$10\frac{7}{8}$	10	$9\frac{3}{4}$	$9\frac{3}{4}$

The exchange rate

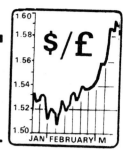

FOREIGN EXCHANGES
BANK SELLS

Austria	20.40	Greece	205	Portugal	220
Belgium	60.45	Ireland	1.08	Spain	204
Canada	2.08	Italy	2,070	Sweden	10.19
Denmark	11.01	Malta	0.535	Switzerland	2.44
France	9.70	Netherlands	3.28	USA	1.585
Germany	2.91	Norway	10.99	Yugoslavia	960

The *exchange rate* is the rate at which one currency can be changed for another. It is the cost of buying one currency with another. Exchange rates are constantly changing: the pound may be worth $1.35 one day and $1.30 the next. There are many factors which determine exchange rates, but government can influence them to some extent if it chooses.

A fall in the exchange rate, ie the pound is worth less in terms of dollars, francs, yen, etc, means:

- Exports (goods and services being sold abroad) become cheaper and easier to sell.
- Imports (goods and services coming into the country from abroad) become more expensive.

The reverse is true if the exchange rate rises: exports become more expensive and imports become cheaper.

Is a fall in the pound good or bad for British business?

---

case study

The effects of a falling pound on Talbot Textiles

After the recent fall in the pound against the dollar and most European currencies, we asked Talbot Textiles export sales manager, Clare Kenney, whether this was good or bad for Talbots.

'There is no easy answer to this question. We export to Europe and the USA so our products will be more competitive in those countries. This might help us sell more. But there are also costs to take into account. We import cotton from the US and some machinery from West Germany. They're all going to be more expensive in the future. The falling pound does mean that competition from imports won't be so intense in the future — that's a plus factor.'

---

questions

1 Explain why a fall in the price of its exports is not necessarily an advantage for Talbot Textiles.
2 Why are Talbot's costs likely to increase as a result of a fall in the pound?
3 Why will competition from imports be less intense in the future?

Inflation and its effects on business

Inflation means a rise in the general level of prices over a period of time. Inflation is measured by looking at an average of prices; within that average some prices are likely to be rising more rapidly than others. Inflation affects business in a number of ways:

- If prices are rising more rapidly in the UK than in other countries, it will make UK exports relatively more expensive, and therefore less attractive, and imports will be more attractive to buyers.
- Costs to the firm will rise if the price of materials is rising. The firm will need either to pass these rising costs on to the buyer or suffer a cut in profit.
- Inflation causes considerable uncertainty. If a contract is signed today for a major engineering project to be completed in two years' time, and inflation increases during that period, the firm may find that it is making a loss on the contract because its production costs have risen.

- Some types of business may benefit through inflation. Property prices, for example, often increase more rapidly than the average rate of inflation, so that those businesses concerned with the property market benefit from rapidly rising prices.
- If firms expect the price of certain materials to rise in the future, they may well be tempted to increase the quantity of stock that they are holding knowing that it will cost them more in six months.

How government aids and controls business: a summary

Business activity	Government measures	*Unit*
Trading	*Support* Enterprise Schemes. Training schemes. Small Firms Service. Assisted areas. Grants. Loans.	Unit 2
	Restraints Company and Partnership Acts. Registrar of Companies. Planning Restrictions	Unit 3

	Support Training Schemes. Job Centres. Information.	Unit 12
Setting up	*Restraints* Health and Safety at Work Act. Employment Acts. Equal opportunities. Employment contracts. Redundancy payments.	Unit 16

Industrial relations	*Support* ACAS, Trade Union legislation.	Unit 13
	Restraints Unfair dismissals. Industrial Tribunals.	

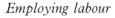

Employing labour	*Support* Export Credits Guarantee Department. Trade fairs. Import restrictions.	Unit 14
	Restraints Monopolies and Mergers Commission. EEC legislation. Consumer	Unit 16
	Protection Acts. Restrictive Practices Act. Advertising Standards Authority. Independent Broadcasting Association.	Unit 14

Health and safety at work act, 1974

- The Act covers all places of work including factories, shops, schools and farms.
- Employees must appoint a Health and Safety Officer to be responsible for the Act being carried out.
- Employers have a responsibility to look after the health and safety of their employees and to take steps to try to prevent accidents occurring, eg having guards on dangerous machinery, providing protective helmets and ear, eye and breathing protection where the circumstances call for them.
- Employees have a responsibility to themselves and to other employees to take steps to prevent accidents occurring.
- There are specific rules for the handling of dangerous substances, such as asbestos and toxic chemicals.

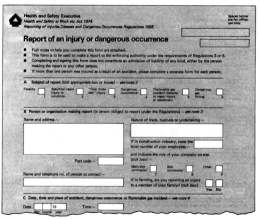

Keith West, a young apprentice, who had been at the firm three months, suffered some permanent damage to his sight. With the support of his union, he took Scott Engineering to court to try and claim compensation for his injury.

The Evidence

The firm claimed that there were notices in the welding area stressing the need to wear safety glasses and that there were plenty of pairs of glasses available at the time of the accident.

The union claimed that Mr West had not been told to wear safety glasses at any stage in his induction training. His supervisor had not stressed the need to wear the glasses. A fellow worker had told Mr West, 'Nobody here bothers to wear the glasses. They're uncomfortable and get in the way'. Few of the workers did, in fact, wear the glasses and the Safety Officer had not reported this fact to the management.

questions

1 In what ways could the following people be blamed for the accident:
   a Keith West,
   b the firm,
   c the supervisor of Keith West,
   d Keith West's fellow workers,
   e the Safety Officer?

2 Who do you think is most responsible for the accident? Explain your answer.

Monopolies, mergers and restrictive practices

Government attempts to prevent businesses restricting competition or engaging in activities which are unfair to the consumer.

The *Monopolies and Mergers Commission* has the power to investigate firms that control 25% or more of the market for a particular good or service within the UK. They can also investigate mergers (joining together of firms) and takeovers which will result in the new firm having 25% or more of the market. The Monopolies and Mergers Commission can make certain recommendations if it is found that the firm is acting against the public interest.

The *Restrictive Practices Court* can investigate cases where firms are engaging in activities which might be regarded as being unfair to the consumer. Such restrictive practices might include *price rings* where a group of firms agree to fix their prices, agreements on *tenders* (bids) for contracts, and firms agreeing to supply only particular retailers.

The *Office of Fair Trading* can refer businesses to both the Monopolies and Mergers Commission and to the Restrictive Practices Court.

The *EEC* also has the power to investigate firms that are operating restrictive practices within the member countries. This makes it possible to take action against some *multinational companies*. These are firms with subsidiaries in a number of different countries.

case study

1 Explain how the road-building industry was engaged in restrictive practices.
2 How might the restrictive practices benefit the road-building companies?
3 Why would the restrictive practices by the road-building firms be against the public interest?
4 What action was taken against the road-building firms?

OFT smashes price ring in roadbuilding tenders

By Roger Cowe

The Office of Fair Trading has uncovered a price fixing ring in the roadbuilding industry. Over 200 firms were yesterday found by the Restrictive Practices Court to have been involved in rigging tenders or fixing prices for the supply of road-making materials including sand, gravel, asphalt and macadam. The customers, who are mainly county councils, may be able to sue the suppliers because of the excess costs they have incurred and because the suppliers have breached the Restrictive Practices Act.

An OFT investigation over several years discovered that prices for materials and haulage were sometimes fixed by local agreement and sometimes suppliers agreed which company would get the job and made sure that company submitted the lowest tender. In some cases minimum orders for materials were also fixed.

The firms involved have had to promise not to operate such agreements in future. If they fail to abide by the promises they will be in contempt of court and liable to fines.

A Happy Eater all clear for THF

TRUSTHOUSE Forte's £190 million acquisition of the Happy Eater restaurants chain and a group of other catering and hotel businesses from Hanson Trust has been given the all clear by the Monopolies and Mergers Commission.

The MMC was called in to investigate the deal in October last year, two months after Trusthouse took control of the former Imperial Group operations.

In addition to the 70 strong Happy Eater chain the deal gave THF control of five Welcome Break motorway service areas, making it the largest operator in the business, together with 30 AnchorHotels and some 85 restaurants and inns.

The Commission was asked to pay particular attention to the implications for competition in the roadside restaurant market where the group already owned the Little Chef chain.

In its report, published yesterday two months ahead of schedule, the Commission concluded unanimously that the merger " may be expected not to operate against the public interest."

The Commission — which carried out a survey into motorists' eating habits as part of the investigation — concluded that although the potential for monopolistic behaviour may have increased as a result of the Happy Eater acquisition there are powerful constraints upon it. Its report points out that a high proportion of motorists are as happy to stop at a pub or other type of outlet as at the Little Chef or Happy Eater restaurants.

1 What takeover was under investigation by the Monopolies and Mergers Commission in the article?
2 Why was the proposed take-over giving cause for concern?
3 Why did the Monopolies and Mergers Commission consider that the take-over would not be against the public interest?

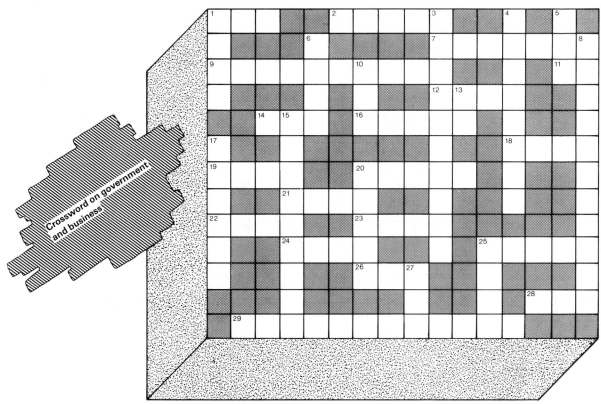

Crossword on government and business

Clues across

1 One way in which government raises revenue. (3)
2 The person involved in 29 across. (5)
7 These will be affected by the £'s exchange rate. (7)
9 One of the main aims of government policy. (10)
11 The bank will remember to pay your rates this way. (initials) (2)
12 A form of income from property which will be liable to tax. (4)
14 An alternative for many young people to unemployment. (initials) (3)
16 A firm must give at least ...... days notice of redundancy after a person has been working with the firm for one month. (5)
18 An Assisted ...... is given special help to try and reduce unemployment. (4)
19 A list of duties to be performed by each person. (4)
20 A firm may be given one of these if it locates in an area of high unemployment. (5)
21 Slang for a march by workers against government policy. (4)
22 Slang for unemployment benefit. (4)
23 A university supported by the government where people learn at home. (4)
24 A multinational car firm. (4)
25 Another way in which government can raise finance. (5)
26 A fee is paid to government for owning a television .... (3)
28 Initials for a government plan to help unemployed adults. (3)
29 A way of buying which will be affected by interest rates. (4–8)

Clues down

1 A course financed in schools by the MSC. (4)
3 Workers who have lost their jobs in declining industries often require this to help them get employment in a new industry. (10)
4 By law, after 13 weeks, an employee is entitled to written details of their employment .... (8)
5 Same as 28 across. (3)
6 Government might lower taxation and increase public expenditure in order to create .... (4)
8 Government may decide to keep a railway line in operation even though it is making a loss because its closure might result in high .... (6–5)
10 Initials of goverment body concerned with employment and training. (3)
13 Her signature is required before it becomes law. (initials) (2)
15 A way of helping exporters advertise their products abroad. (5–4)
17 Government may raise interest rates to reduce the amount spent on this way of buying goods. (6)
20 Part of government policy is to encourage a greater output of ...... and services. (5)
25 Sets of things sold at auction. (4)
27 Government may consult with this body representing the interests of workers. (initials) (3)

Answers to clues on page 231.

Summary of key words and ideas

- *Inflation* is a rise in the general level of prices over a period of time.
- If inflation is higher in the UK than in other countries it will make it more difficult to sell goods abroad, and imports will appear more attractive.
- Government uses the level of tax and the level of public spending to influence the economy. An increase in public spending and a decrease in tax will result in increased spending by consumers.
- *Interest* is the cost of borrowing money. An increase in the rate of interest will make it more expensive to borrow and this will tend to reduce credit and hire-purchase spending.
- The *exchange rate* is the rate at which one currency can be changed for another. An increase in the exchange rate will make exports more expensive and imports relatively cheaper. A fall in the exchange rate will make it easier for firms to export, but their import costs will also rise.
- Government both supports and restrains business activity. It supports it in terms of finance, training schemes, and helping exporting firms. It places restraint upon firms in terms of the conditions of employment, and practices, which may be unfair to the consumer.
- The *Monopolies and Mergers Commission* investigates businesses which control 25% or more of the market for a good or service and can recommend action to be taken if it is found that the firm is acting against the public interest.
- The *Restrictive Practices Court* investigates business activities which are regarded as being unfair to the consumer.

Suggestions for coursework

1 The Budget is announced each year in March. Collect as many details and reports as possible of the last Budget. Describe the changes which are being made in taxation and spending and say how they might affect businesses. Try and include comments from the CBI, the TUC and individual businesses.

2 For your school or a local business do a survey to see how the Health and Safety Act is carried out. Try and obtain an interview with the Health and Safety Officer. Say what the main causes of accidents are and what measures are taken to try to prevent them from occurring.

3 Watch out for reports of take-over bids or restrictive practices which have been referred to the Monopolies and Mergers Commission or the Office of Fair Trading. Why has the firm been referred? What was the outcome? Who benefits and who loses out as a result of the decision?

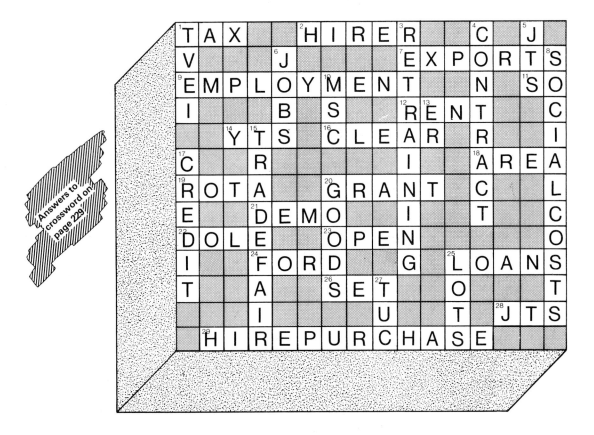

Answers to crossword on page 229

The crossword contains the following filled letters:

Row 1: ¹T A X ²H I R E R ⁴C ⁵J
Row 2: V ⁶J ⁷E X P O R T ⁸S
Row 3: ⁹E M P L O Y ¹⁰M E N T N ¹¹S O
Row 4: I B S ¹²R ¹³E N T C
Row 5: ¹⁴Y ¹⁵T S ¹⁶C L E A R R I
Row 6: ¹⁷C R I ¹⁸A R E A
Row 7: ¹⁹R O T A ²⁰G R A N T C L
Row 8: E ²¹D E M O I T C
Row 9: ²²D O L E ²³O P E N N O
Row 10: I ²⁴F O R D G ²⁵L O A N S
Row 11: T A S ²⁶S E ²⁷T O T
Row 12: I U T ²⁸J T S
Row 13: ²⁹H I R E P U R C H A S E

Test questions

1 'One main objective of government economic policy is to have a low rate of inflation'.
   a What is meant by inflation?
   b Name two other main objectives of government economic policy besides low inflation.
   c What problems could a high level of inflation cause for a business?

2 The Government decides to abolish VAT on household electrical goods made in the UK.
   a What is VAT?
   b Describe two possible results of this action.
   c Why might the Government take this action?

3 The Government announces that it intends to increase its spending on roadbuilding by £300 million.
   a Describe two direct effects that this will have upon the roadbuilding industry.
   b Describe what the indirect effect of this might be on the whole economy (assuming that government does not make any other changes).

4 'Interest Rate rises by 2%'.
   a What is meant by an interest rate?
   b Give two reasons why this might be harmful to businesses.
5 The exchange rate of the pound against the French franc has fallen from 10 francs to the pound to 9 francs to the pound. How would this fall affect:
   a someone from the UK going on holiday in France,
   b a firm that exports a large part of their output to France,
   c a firm importing components from France?
6 Describe two ways in which government attempts to assist people who are unemployed find another job.
7 Describe two ways in which government attempts to help firms increase their exports.
8 Describe four precautions which the Health and Safety Act insists upon in a workshop.

Extension questions

1 The Monopolies and Mergers Commission can recommend measures to be taken against firms which are shown to be 'acting against the public interest'. Describe two ways in which a firm might be considered to be acting against the public interest.
2 The Restrictive Practices Court investigates unfair trade practices such as price rings and agreements on tenders.
   a What is a price ring?
   b Why might a price ring be unfair to the consumer?
   c How would agreements on tenders operate?
   d How could both price rings and tender agreements be beneficial to the firms involved in them?